CONQUISTADORA

A princess, a slave, a conqueror

A woman who changed the world

Sean Wheeler

Foreword

I first became peripherally aware of La Malinche, Malinali or Dona Marina as she is called by the Spaniards, on vacation trips to Mexico. Subsequent to this, I became more aware of her role in the Spanish conquest of the Aztec Empire. Hernan Cortes himself credits her, after God, with his success in the conquest of what is now Mexico. Her story is a remarkable one, intertwined as it is with one of history's great landmarks and turning points. Her resilience in the face of her fall from princess to slave, then to be lifted up on a pedestal by the conquistadors is remarkable. Her ability to learn multiple languages and use them to negotiate positive alliances and outcomes for the Spanish was clearly what facilitated their success. It is unlikely that Cortes could have achieved his remarkable victory without her brilliance. Setting out with less than 600 men to do battle with an empire capable of putting several millions under arms the odds were against him. Even the massive technological advantage of horses, guns and steel would not have made the conquest possible without the hundreds of thousands of native warriors who allied themselves with the Spanish cause.

Her story is reasonably well documented during the years of the conquest but very little is known for certain of her early life and even her post conquest life is sketchy. All the histories

I could find reference to were about Cortes and the conquest. Her contribution has certainly been acknowledged by historians, yet I couldn't find any adult English language accounts of her story. I found a young adult book: 'Malinche, Slave Princess of Cortez' by Gloria Duran, Linnet Books 1993; and a children's picture book: 'La Malinche, The Princess who helped Cortes conquer the Aztec Empire by Francisco Serrano, illustrated by Pablo Serrano, Groundwood Books/House of Anansi Press. These were useful to me, as was the wonderfully written 'Conquistador, Hernan Cortes, King Montezuma, and the Last Stand of the Aztecs' by Buddy Levy, Bantam Books 2009.

Subsequent to finishing my version of the story I found an illustrated version of her story by Rodrigue Levesque and a text by Laura Esquivel, so my undertaking was not as unique as I'd imagined!

I decided to write this book to honour one of the most remarkable 'unknown' women (at least outside of Mexico) of history. This is not a history book, but where possible I have kept to the recorded history as far as I was able to access it. For the purposes of the narrative, I have invented numerous characters and events, primarily in her early life.

The story itself is unbelievable. Were it a pure work of fiction, I would have been challenged to believe that a small navy could be constructed and carried over mountains to achieve domination of the lakes controlled by the Aztecs. Likewise, the sheer numerical imbalance makes it so unlikely that victory could have been achieved. It isn't possible to know how to weigh the contribution the technology, smallpox, and the remarkable skills of Dona Marina made to the victories. In hope of achieving a readable text that isn't just one battle after another I have simplified the campaigns undertaken by the Spanish conquistadors. I have chosen to call this story 'Conquistadora' as I think this woman truly belongs alongside the likes of Cortes and Pizarro in the pantheon of great explorer/conquerors. I hope it amuses and to some degree enlightens. To aid the reader in keeping track of the multiple personages in the story there follows a list of the key characters, and Aztec places and deities.

List of major characters (In order of their appearance in the narrative):

Acalan (fictional): Malinali's father and ruler of a modest Mayan town near Xaltipan one of multiple Maya fiefdoms subjected to Aztec rule.

Eleuia (fictional): Malinali's wet-nurse, primary nurturer and teacher.

Malinali (c.1500-c.1529): Born a princess, sold into slavery, variously called Malinali, La Malinche, Chantico and finally when baptised Dona Marina.

Xoco (fictional): Head midwife who supervised Malinali's birth.

Cimatl (fictional): Malinali's mother

Chiconahui (fictional): Female overseer of lord to whom Malinali was sold.

Hernan Cortes (1485-1547): Spanish conquistador who led an expedition that caused the fall of the Aztec Empire and brought large portions of what is now mainland Mexico under the rule of the king of Castile in the early 16th century.

Antonio de Alaminos (1482-?): One of the pre-eminent navigators of his era.

Pedro de Alvarado (1485-1541): Conquistador who served with Cortes as one of his captains. Famously impulsive but brave. Went on to become the governor of much of what is now Central America.

Jeronimo de Aguilar (1489-1531): was a Franciscan friar born in Ecija, Spain. Aguilar was sent to Panama to serve as a missionary. He was later shipwrecked on the Yucatan

Peninsula in 1511 and captured by the Maya. In 1519 Cortes rescued Aguilar and engaged him as a translator.

Bartolome de Olmedo (c.1485-1524): was a Mercedarian friar who accompanied Cortes in the conquest of Mexico.

Alonso Hernandez Puertocarrero (before 1495-1523): Fought alongside Cortes and was initially gifted the slave woman Malinali but Cortes, on realising her skills, took her back. Puertocarrero was later sent to Spain bearing gifts and letters for King Charles of Castile.

Montezuma (c.1466-1520): referred to retroactively in European sources as Moctezuma II, was the ninth Emperor of the Aztec Empire (also known as the Mexica Empire), reigning from 1502 or 1503 to 1520.

Tendile (Dates unknown): The man who first officially greets Cortes on behalf of the Aztec Empire was a man of importance and his story exists in snippets across multiple historical records.

Diego Velazquez (1465 – 1524) was a Spanish Conquistador and the first governor of Cuba. In 1511 he led the successful conquest and colonization of Cuba. Initially a friend and business partner of Cortes, they later became rivals.

Gonzalo de Sandoval (1497– 1528): Spanish conquistador, was Cortes' most loyal Captain. He participated in both the conquest of Mexico and later expedition to what is now Honduras.

Juan de Escalante (c.1479-1519): Trusted Lieutenant of Cortes, was made governor of the newly established town of Vera Cruz.

Xicotenga the younger and elder (Dates not known): Leaders of Tlaxcala, initially hostile to the Spanish they later became their most loyal and useful allies.

Itzel (fictional): Cholulan noblewoman who befriends Dona Marina and later lets slip Cholulan plans for an ambush.

Bernal Diaz (c.1492-1584) was a Spanish conquistador, who participated as a soldier in the conquest of the Aztec Empire under Hernán Cortés and late in his life wrote an account of the events.

Diego de Ordaz (1480-1532) De Ordaz accompanied Cortes on his expedition of conquest to the Mexican mainland. Together with two comrades, he was the first European to climb to the top of the volcano Popocatepetl. on October 22, 1525, Charles V issued a decree permitting him to use a coat-of-arms featuring a view of the volcano.

Cacama (1483–1520) was the tlatoani (ruler) of Texcoco, the second most important city of the Aztec Empire. He was the nephew of Montezuma the Aztec emperor.

Qualpopoca (?- 1520) Aztec general responsible for the killing of the governor of Vera Cruz, Juan de Escalante, in a cunningly contrived ambush.

Cristóbal de Olid (1487–1524) was a Spanish adventurer and conquistador who played a significant part in the conquest of Mexico and Honduras. He acted at times as the captain of Cortes' personal body guard and on more than one occasion may have saved his leader's life.

Martin Lopez (?- 1573) Despite having no previous naval experience he designed and built a small fleet of cannon armed ships that proved decisive in the battle for Tenochtitlan.

Panfilo de Narvaez (c.147? – 1528) Spanish conquistador and adventurer sent by Diego Valazquez in a vain attempt to bring Cortes to heel. Despite a 3 to 1 advantage in men he was defeated.

Cuitlahuac (?-1520) Aztec emperor who succeeded Montezuma, he ruled just 80 days, perhaps dying from small pox that had been introduced to the New World by an African suffering from the disease who was part of Panfilo de Narvaez' expedition to capture Cortés.

Julian de Alderete (1490-c.1525) Sent from Castile to be the royal treasurer. His primary role was to ensure that the king received his 'Royal Fifth'. The ship he arrived on carried good stores of gunpowder and weapons which were much needed at the time.

Cuauhtémoc (?-1521) was the Aztec ruler from 1520 to 1521, making him the last Aztec Emperor. The name Cuauhtemoc means "one who has descended like an eagle" and is commonly rendered in English as "Descending Eagle", as in the moment when an eagle folds its wings and plummets down to strike its prey. This is a name that implies aggressiveness and determination.

Garci de Holguin (1490-?) Captained one of the brigantines used by Cortes to control the lakes of the Triple Alliance. Along with Gonzalo Sandoval he captured the Aztec emperor Cuauhtemoc as he sought to escape from Tenochtitlan.

Catalina Suarez Marcaida de Cortes (c.1498- 1522) was married to Hernan Cortes and died in mysterious circumstances not long after arriving in Mexico.

Diego de Almagro (c. 1475 –1538), also known as El Adelantado and El Viejo, was a Spanish sea captain who later became a conquistador known for his exploits in western South America. He participated with Francisco Pizarro in the Spanish conquest of the Inca Empire in what is modern day Peru.

Patli (fictional) Head of Dona Marina's household in her final years.

Gil González Dávila or **Gil González de Ávila** (b. 1480 – 1526) was a Spanish conquistador and the first European to explore present-day Nicaragua.

Some significant Aztec places and words

Aztlán is the ancestral home of the Aztec peoples. Astekah is the Nahuatl word for "people from Aztlan". Historians have speculated about the possible location of Aztlan and tend to place it either in northwestern Mexico or the Southwestern United States although whether Aztlan represents a real location or is purely mythological is a matter of debate.

Chalchiuhtlicue (from *chālchihuitl* "jade" and *cuēitl* "skirt") ("She of the Jade Skirt") is an **Aztec** deity of water, rivers, seas, streams, storms, and baptism. Chalchiuhtlicue is associated with fertility, and she is the patroness of childbirth. Chalchiuhtlicue was highly revered in Aztec culture at the time of the Spanish conquest.

Coatzacoalcos comes from a Nahuatl word meaning "site of the Snake" or "where the snake hides." According to the legend, this is where the god Quetzalcoatl made his final journey to the sea in around 999 and he made his promise to return.

Huitzilopochtli, also spelled Uitzilopochtli, also called Xiuhpilli ("Turquoise Prince") and Totec ("Our Lord"), Aztec sun and war god, one of the two principal deities of Aztec religion, often represented in art as either a hummingbird or an eagle.

Mictlan is the underworld of Aztec mythology. Most people who die would travel to Mictlan, although other possibilities exist. Mictlan consists of nine distinct levels. The journey from the first level to the ninth is difficult and takes four years, The dead must pass many challenges, such as crossing a mountain range where the mountains crash into each other, a field with wind that blows flesh-scraping knives, and a river of blood with fearsome jaguars.

Nahuatl primary language of the Aztecs or Mexicano is a language or, by some definitions, a group of languages. Varieties of Nahuatl are spoken by about 1.7 million Nahua peoples most of whom live mainly in Central Mexico and have smaller populations in the United States.

Quetzalcoatl to the Aztecs, Quetzalcoatl was, as his name indicates, a feathered serpent. He was a creator deity having contributed essentially to the creation of mankind. According to Aztec legend he had been banished "To the East" but would return one day to claim his rightful place.

Tenochtitlan Founded sometime in the 1300's as the capital of the Aztec Empire. At the time of the Spanish arrival it was by far the largest city in the world. Sited on a network of lakes it was accessible only by water or long causeways. After its partial destruction the pre-cursor to modern day Mexico City was built over the ruins.

Triple Alliance The Aztec Empire or the Triple Alliance was an alliance of three Nahua city states: Mexico/Tenochtitlan, Texcoco, and Tlacopan. These three city-states ruled the area in and around the Valley of Mexico from 1428 until the combined forces of the Spanish conquistadores and their native allies defeated them in 1521.

The alliance was formed from the victorious factions of a civil war fought between the city of Azcapotzalco and its former tributary provinces. Despite the initial conception of the empire as an alliance of three self-governed city-states, the capital Tenochtitlan became dominant militarily. By the time the Spanish arrived in 1519, the lands of the alliance were effectively ruled from Tenochtitlan, while other partners of the alliance had taken subsidiary roles.

Tlalocan is described in several Aztec codices as a paradise, ruled over by the rain deity Tlaloc and his consort Chalchiuhtlicue. It absorbed those who died through drowning or lightning, or as a consequence of diseases associated with the rain deity.

Xipe Totec In Aztec mythology, Xipe Totec (the Flayed One) was a life/death/rebirth deity, god of agriculture and vegetation, the east, spring, goldsmiths, silversmiths, deadly warfare, the seasons, and the earth.

Yax tun Jade or Greenstone much prized for its translucent green colour and its utility in making weapons.

Chapter one Born a princess

"Come Father sit by me and write for me my story. Beg Our Lord's forgiveness for the sins I disclose, for I have played my part in the shedding of rivers of blood.

The circumstances of my birth are, as is the way of such things, surrounded in mystery and myth, enveloped in a foggy cloud of half remembered, half-forgotten events and people. The tellings of the story that my mind remembers are at times in agreement, at others as if they were two or more separate tales. All I can truly claim as fact is that I lay here telling you this story now, that my lungs still hold breath, and my eyes can still see the steady dance of the sunlight as it makes its leisurely way across my room. I feel the heat of the fever in my blood, and I know what this redness on my skin means. I bless you Father for taking this time with me to record my story. The rest is like alternate worlds that shatter and split into myriad alike but different images. Perhaps much is old wives' tales. I have stood abreast the wave of the future and seen more changes than can be held in one person's mind. But wait, we will come to that soon enough, forgive my digressions, let's start at the start.

I can tell you about my parents. My father was a warm and caring man who knew how to give and receive love. He was a strong leader of our people, firm and fair in his judgements and admired by most. More the pity that he left me so early. My mother was a strong and unbending woman and though I cannot say I ever loved her, nor she me, I am grateful to her for the accident of my birth and the strength of my spine and will. I was born a princess and by virtue of my birth should have expected an easier life. The words have different meanings in different cultures, for I too have experienced more than one, but though the words change from king and queen to chief and chieftainess to lord and lady their meaning is the same: those who by merit of birth alone have dominion over others. Of course, there are good and evil in all classes of life from the highest born to the lowliest of slaves. Power and privilege are simply magnifiers, the potential for good or evil remains inherent.

I was born in the season of the ripe corn. The night was cloudy with a cold wind howling down from the heights, brief valleys in the mountains of thunderclouds revealed the light of a blood red moon from time to time. At the moment of my birth the clouds parted, and the eerie red light of the moon ran the roads of the city with flowing fresh sacrificial blood. Every dog in the city turned its gaping maw to the moon and howled, deep in the jungles the jaguar tensed every sinew and displayed their fearsome teeth...

Or I was born on a still and inauspicious night. I was there, but I can't remember.

My birth was easy, I am told, and I came into this world willingly without causing the mother of my birth too much pain. I am told when informed of what lay between my legs, she had no wish to hold me and commanded that I be passed over to the wet-nurse who was to feed me and take up my care. So it was that I gazed into the soft deep eyes of my real mother.

Later, when I had enough of her rich milk, so I am told, I was taken to meet my father. The lord (or king or chieftain, we've been through that) Acalan was apparently better pleased than his wife to be presented with a daughter. He took me from Eleuia's gentle arms and held me for himself. Gazing down into my scrunched-up baby face he gave me my first name.

"She shall be called Malinali, the one of the waving grasses" he is alleged to have declared. *"And as my first-born she is to be accorded all the adoration and privilege of a princess."*

This may have been a most fortuitous declaration on his part and may have protected me, at least to begin with, from any malice that my mother's disappointment may have brewed. The next part was no different for me than for any other new-born infant. Though wrapped in a finer quality of cloth than others, the ceremony was always the same:

Eleuia and Xoco the attendant midwife, would have taken me out to the grand house's central courtyard. There a bowl filled with water that had been fortified with spells and incantations lay in wait. Xoco would have taken me from my mother's arms and knelt down to the bowl. Dipping two fingers into the bowl she would touch the special liquid to my forehead, then my chest, and finally to my lips, ensuring that a few drops were taken into my mouth.

"Chalchiuhtlicue! Cleanse thy heart; make it fine, good. May she guide your conduct and make it good."

Xoco would then have taken up the cord that had bound me within my birth mother's body, and a specially carved spindle, and carefully buried them under the great metate stone that had been cleaned of the scraps of ground corn for this ceremony.

Eleuia, whose name means *"she who wishes good for everyone"*, loved me as her own. She had borne three children herself, none of whom had survived beyond the age of one year. Later, when I had acquired the first of my tongues, she explained to me the circumstances of my birth. My birth mother, Cimatl, showed no interest in me, her focus was on conceiving a son to continue the noble lineage; she herself was of noble blood at least equal to that of Acalan, but she was aware that being succeeded by a son was crucial for both of them. Eleuia, as was her wont, seemed to forgive my birth mother of her coldness, I for my part came to not care. Eleuia and my father Acalan showered me with more than enough love and affection for any child.

We lived in one of the many small houses clustered around the great house of my father. As well as caring for me, Eleuia continued her general duties which primarily consisted of helping with the cooking and serving of food at the great house. At first, as she worked, she would tie the me to her chest, stopping as required to suckle me on her fulsome breasts. It was only later when I had held a child of my own in my arms that I realised what a gift I must have been to this kind and loving woman who had brought me up.

She was well pleased when the lord Acalan would call her over to enquire of the child's well-being, and at times hold me in his arms.

I was healthy. I grew strong and soon showed signs that I would be considered a great beauty. Soon enough my legs had found their way to the ground and I was able to walk alongside Eleuia as she carried out her duties. Eleuia was delighted at the speed with which I learnt to speak and even to read the picture and sound scripts that told of the gods and the family's history. Later when I was strong and steady enough to carry small dishes I was proud to work alongside Eli.

I cannot remember Father what age I was when I met the serpent. I think I must have been 3 or 4 but I cannot be certain. I had wandered off on my own, something that I did often much to Eli's frustration. If I could not hear or in my stubborn way, would not answer her calls, she would send some of the other servants out to look for me. When I was discovered in my own dream-world I would be taken back to the compound and given a good scolding. Eli never struck me. I was normally within earshot of the royal compound but sometimes I strayed further afield.

I had been following a bird, a really pretty little hummingbird with a bright shining green chest that was dipping its long beak into the sweet cups of various flowers. I knew that hummingbirds were special. I had learnt that Huitzilopochtli himself was often in the form of a hummingbird. Some also had said to me that the hummingbird was the soul of a warrior that stayed to look after his people. Regardless of these and other tales I was fascinated by birds of all kinds. How miraculous a bird is Father! It can lift itself up in to the sky and free itself from the weight of its own body. Hummingbirds are especially miraculous; their little wings beat so fast that they can't be seen and I have never seen one at rest. Without thinking I followed this delightful creature far from the compound.

Finally, after I know not how long, this little visitor from the heavens flitted off and I could follow him no more. I was tired so I sat cross-legged beneath a ceiba tree to rest awhile even though I knew that there would be a search party after me soon enough. It was very pleasant resting my back against the smooth trunk of the tree listening to the insects sing their songs. I must have dozed off because I awoke with a start and realised that there was something in my lap.

Looking down I saw that there was a bright yellow serpent curled up in my lap. The creature seemed unworried by me, and even though I knew that many of our serpents had venomous bites I was likewise unafraid. This serpent was unusual, it had scales above its eyes that looked for all the world like eyelashes on a person. I gazed into its eyes and in my childish imagination I imagined that it was trying to tell me something. I don't know how long I stared into its round golden eyes with their strange upright dark entrances before I was woken from my reverie by a shout.

A servant from the household stood before me with a shocked, worried, look on her face. I knew it must be time to go home, so I calmly and gently lifted my serpent friend from my lap and placed him softly on the earth by the tree. All this time the servant was staring at me with wide-open eyes. As I knew would happen, Eli gave me a good telling off when I arrived home.

Often as Eli and I served the lord and lady, Acalan would call me over:

"So, little one what have you been up to today?" he would enquire with a soft twinkle in his black eyes.

"I've been helping Eli with making the tortilla my lord. And I've been learning how to read the sacred scripts and how to count my numbers." I would reply.

"That's good my little one, keep helping Eli and studying, and one day I may take you with me to the great city" was often his response.

And so for the first but not the last time I learnt patience; one day was a long time coming.

I was very excited at this prospect of making such a journey. I had heard much about the great city of Tenochtitlan, the city of the lakes, the great centre for the Aztec. I had often wondered if I would ever get to travel so far to see it.

"Why does my mama not take me onto her knee the way my lord Acalan does?" I asked Eli one day.

"Ah, my beloved, she was certain that you would be a boy when she was pregnant. All the omens pointed to it being so. She was very disappointed when your nature was revealed."

I nodded but thought that it was silly of my mother. I knew that I had it in me to do great things. Already, at only aged six, I knew that I was further ahead in my studies than all the other children born in the same season, even the boys. I was fluent with a wide vocabulary in my own Maya tongue and was now learning the Nahuatl of the Tenochtitlan overlords. Eli sometimes said that I had the ear of the boldest parrot and once I heard a word I knew it forever. She would often praise me for the quality of my weaving, even at this age she would leave me to confidently complete complicated patterns unsupervised.

From an early age I loved to swim. Most days I would go down to the Coatzacoalcos river with my little tribe of friends, most of whom were boys. There I would dive straight into the river even if its current was running swiftly. I was the strongest swimmer of all the young ones and could hold my breath longest underwater and swim the furthest on a single breath. I loved the freedom of being in the water, I felt as though I were some magical creature as I moved freely in the water just like a bird flying through the air. The Coatzacoalcos river has very special properties, it is said that it got its name, which means 'the place where the serpent hides' when the god Quetzalcoatl was on a raft made of serpent skins as he sailed out towards the great ocean. I felt as though every swim made me stronger and sharpened my mind.

Finally in my eighth year I was summoned to my father's chamber.

"I am journeying to the lake city for the twenty-day ceremony of Tlacaxipehualizti, to ensure that Xipe Totec will bless our crops and our seeds will grow. I wish to take you with me so that you can see the Great City."

"Yes, yes, my lord, thank you. When will we be leaving?"

For some reason this made him smile that smile that crinkled his cheeks and made his eyes sparkle.

"At the rising of the morning sun" he replied.

That night as I lay on my sleeping mat I couldn't stop my thoughts from racing. The great city! The stories I'd been told made it sound like it was truly the city of the Gods. Very few people had been to the great city before and I couldn't think of anyone except my father and his attendant slaves and servants who had made the journey. Eli had told me that the journey would take eight passages of the sun and would involve climbing mountains to a great height to reach the bowl of the lakes. I had heard many things about the Aztec. I knew they were great warriors and had conquered my tribe and all others right down to the great water and further- for more land rods than could be counted. Eli had told me that there were great pyramids and temples that would make our local ones seem like children's toys. I thought it likely that dear sweet Eli who had never been anywhere outside our city walls was laying it all on a bit thick. At last the soft hands of sleep wrapped around me and carried me off to the world of dreams.

This is my dream:

I was standing on the shore of a great body of water, so immense that it went on beyond the reach of my eyes. As I stood, straining my eyes against the horizon, a monstrous serpent appeared in the distance. I could see its head standing high above the azure waters that stretched before me. The head was not like any other snake I had seen. It was covered with white and black feathers that stood out like a halo from its huge head. I trembled. The snake came closer and closer and its bulk blotted out the light from the rising sun. Still I stood. I faced the strange creature and for a moment could see my own reflection trapped in the cold amber of its eyes. And then without a hiss the gigantic serpent swung its open jaws around me and my world went dark.

"Mali! Mali! It's time to rise, the lord's men are readying his litter and gathering provisions for the journey."

I awoke with a start to find Eli standing over my mat shaking my shoulders. I was still befuddled by my dream but quickly arose and washed my face before feasting on the tortilla and fruits that Eli had prepared for me. Eli handed me a small bundle of treats for the journey and embraced me, whispering in my ear *"travel safely my daughter, and bring me back the true stories of the Aztec city"*. I made my way to the big house where my father's caravan was ready to set out on the journey.

"Ah Mali, come and sit next to me, my warriors won't notice your weight, they are strong and steadfast."

I took my place next to Acalan on the cushion festooned palanquin which was soon uplifted by four of the warriors who were to be their bearers for the first part of the journey. Another eight warriors would jog alongside ready to take their turn in consuming the honour of lifting their lord. In the middle of the warriors who weren't currently carrying the palanquin were five slaves joined by a rope umbilical. As well as the warriors, there were a score or more of servants and porters carrying provisions and gifts for the mighty Mexica lords they would meet at the city of the lakes. As they set off I could see Eli watching our departure intently; further back in the shadows of a doorway I thought I could see the mother of my birth.

The journey began uneventfully. I got used to the slight swaying of the palanquin and soon learnt the pattern of the journeying. We would travel from sunrise to the highest point of the sun in the sky, then rest under the shade of trees, or on one occasion the house of one of the minor nobility whose land lay in our path. Later, we would take to the path again and travel to the end of daylight.

As we journeyed Acalan told me the history of our people and the troubles and benefits that the Mexica overlords had brought them.

"Our people fought as bravely as any people under the sun. The streets ran with their blood and the skies echoed with the cries of widows and orphans but to no avail. The Mexica were great in number, their warriors well-armed, their discipline unbreakable and their generals full of cunning and deceit." He told me.

"Oh lord, that sounds terrible, they must be evil."

"No, my little one, there are no folk under the sun who are wholly good or evil. Since then we have had generations of peace, the Mexica have built fine roads and trade between all the peoples of the land has made us all the richer. Yes, we must pay our tributes in corn and gold and slaves, but in the end we are probably better off than before."

I was silent for a while then as I absorbed this knowledge, letting it soak deep into my soul. This was the first time that I had left the place of my birth. In truth these Aztec or Mexica as they were sometimes called sounded truly powerful and in complete mastery of all they surveyed. Yet I have always thirsted for knowledge of this rich and terrible world that we enter at the moment of our birth, so my apprehension was tempered by my excitement at what I imagined lay ahead.

As the caravan wound its way we climbed steadily. Some of the sections were steep. The relays of warriors would swap places more frequently to ensure that none were too exhausted by the steep slopes and increasing thinness of the very air around them. As we passed the narrowest sections of the path, I found myself clutching my father's knee as I looked down the precipitous drop to the valley below. One slip by a bearer and we would surely see if we had wings! Despite it being one of the hottest months of the year the temperatures steadily dropped, and at night I had to wrap myself in several layers of thick woven blankets. From the highest point of our journey I could see the two fuming mountains: Popocatepetl, smoking mountain, and his sister known as Iztaccihautl, the white woman.

On the morning of the eighth day we began to descend from the heights into the verdant bowl of the plains beneath the peaks. From our great height it was as though I were a great eagle about to swoop down on the city below. I could see more and more houses, and in the distance the pyramids of the sun and moon rose like great blue and red spectres from the landscape. The path was now paved and we entered onto a great causeway that traversed the mirror-like surface of a lake. To each side of this main causeway branches like those of a mighty tree spread out leading to gardens, houses, and minor temples. Canals wove like some climbing plant amongst all these branches. Canoes loaded with people or goods swarmed along the canals, moving the goods and workers that kept this thriving city pulsing and beating with life.

The closer our journey took us to the heart of this city the grander the buildings became. I was amazed to see several palaces that made those of my lord Acalan's seem as insignificant as that of a minor merchant. I had been so busy looking at the buildings surrounding the causeway that I barely noticed that the porters carrying our palanquin had come to a halt. Standing in front of them was a group of men who can only have been of noble blood. Each was wonderfully attired in finely woven clothes adorned with thread in patterns of blue, black, and red; around their waists were the xiuhtlulpill that denoted nobility; several carried oval shields decorated with brightly coloured feathers.

"Father how did this great city come to be built here? Why did they build it on the little islands of the lake? Surely there must have been better and easier places to build?" I asked.

My father smiled at me; he was well used to my never ending questions as I sought to understand all that the world laid before me.

"The Aztec, or Mexica as some call them, left their homeland of Aztlan at the direction of their god, Huitzilopochtli. Huitzilopochtli directed them to build where they saw an eagle perched on a cactus, eating a snake. When they saw this exact scene on an island, they interpreted it as a sign from their god and founded Tenochtitlan."

"Where is Aztlan father and why did the Aztec leave to come here?"

"Even the Aztec themselves don't know exactly where it is, somewhere far away to the North and West. As to why they left it is simple, they were just following the direction of the god Huitzilopochtli."

I was about to ask more questions so that I could understand this long migration but my father hushed me as he needed to focus his attention meeting with the Aztec delegation.

At a word from Acalan, the porters gently placed the palanquin on the ground and laid out cloths for him to step onto. I was well used to the notion that a lord's feet should never touch the raw earth or even a paved surface. With a wave of his hand Acalan bade me to wait at the palanquin while he stepped forward to be greeted by the Aztec party. Though I couldn't hear the conversations I could see the gifts being exchanged by both parties. Even I could see that the gifts Acalan received were grander and more beautiful than those he gave. There were necklaces and bracelets of bright turquoise, others of jade, bowls and plates painted with vibrant colours, and a golden chalice. I could see him gesturing towards the five slaves that had been brought along; though they didn't change hands at that moment.

When this exchange was complete the Aztec nobles left behind a small group of servants who were to guide Acalan and our party to our allocated accommodation.

My father turned to me and the rest of the entourage saying:

"We have been welcomed into the city and will be guided to our houses. The nobles who welcomed us seem well enough pleased with our gifts and tomorrow we will be taken to the great square for the beginning of the ceremonies. Tonight we will keep our own council, sleep well, and prepare for the morrow."

They were led down one of the branches that came off the main causeway to a house that was of similar proportions to their palace at home. The servants immediately began the work of grinding corn, slaughtering a turkey, and preparing beans and other vegetables; all of which had been laid on for them by their hosts. I was about to help the servants with the work but my father intervened.

"No little one, on this trip you are here as my daughter and will accompany me to all events. Leave the food preparation and other household tasks to the servants."

That night I slept well, I do not remember my traverse through the dream-world; our journey here on the mortal plane had been long and despite little physical exertion on my part, I found myself quickly gone from consciousness.

Chapter two: Ritual and reversal

As I look back on that time all those years ago Father I see it with different eyes. The long passage of time has not dimmed my outward eyes but the eyes I use to look back on my past are not the same as those I experienced it with. Now, with the light of my lord, Christ the redeemer, shining down on me, the religion, and rituals of the Aztec, and even of my own people, seem savage and false.

The next days followed a repeating pattern of ceremony and prayer. For day after day there were stories of the god Xipe Totec: God of the cycle of death and rebirth, bringer of growth and Spring, master of all warfare, the flayed one, these followed by long hours of ritual chanting and the singing of special songs. Of course I knew of Xipe Totec, but here I heard the full story of his role in the survival of the people. He was responsible for the bringing of the rains, for the germination of seeds and the bountifulness of the land. He had indeed flayed himself to feed the first people. As well as this essential role in the survival of the tribes he was said to be the inventor of warfare itself. As I listened to these stories which were told in Nahuatl and translated into Maya for me by my father, I came to see that life and death were joined together and that one was not possible without the other. I took great interest in the language of the Aztec and papa was amazed at the speed with which I learnt Nahuatl; I would not let a single word go by without understanding its meaning. Perhaps dear sweet Eli was right and my ears had special magic. Dear Eli, it was only as I lay down to sleep at night that I had time to truly miss my mother.

On the fifteenth day of the ceremony there was the first of the ritual sacrifices. In preparation a dozen of the tribute slaves were taken to the top of the temple. One by one they were laid across the great stone and the priests would approach them with incantations. Each slave was led to the stone by priests. From where I stood they seemed to be calm and not resisting what was about to happen to them. Burning herbs wafted their smoke, and incantations were chanted over and over again. And then there was silence. The head priest took an obsidian knife and briefly held it over the sacrificial offering with further prayers. The crowd of many thousands drew breath and held. Then the knife plunged to open up the slave's chest cavity. Reaching in, the high priest pulled out the still beating heart of the sacrificial man and held it up to the sun. The blood that flowed in rivers down the stone ran into channels and was collected to be spread on the fields to ensure good growth and a bountiful harvest. The other priests took out blades and carefully peeled the skin off the body. The skins were then decorated with feathers and beads before being worn by the assembled priests.

When all were duly sacrificed, the dozen skin-clad priests were ready for the warrior games. These dozen priests were led down to one of the many plazas where they began a mock combat with a group of warriors. I who had not yet in all my years witnessed real fighting could tell that this was more like a dance. Indeed blows were exchanged, but it seemed that the swinging arm was each time slowed down just as the blade neared an opponent's body. None the less it was a grand spectacle. The skin-clad priests gained the upper hand in this mock battle and soon all of the brightly clad warriors were laying on the stones of the courtyard feigning death.

"You see Mali, the sacrifice brings victory in battle, and the blood of the sacrificed makes the fields grow well and new life spread."

Each of the remaining days of the festival now followed this format except for the final day. On the ultimate day, only one person was led to the sacrificial stone. This was a particularly handsome and strong looking warrior. His hair was shoulder length and his features were both strong and fine. Over his muscled body he wore the cloak and feathers of a much-revered warrior.

"That doesn't look like a slave my lord" I exclaimed.

"No he's not, replied papa *"he is a warrior chosen from among the elite guards who has been treated like a king for a year. There has been nothing he might desire that has been denied him. All year long seven slave girls have provided him with every possible service. Now he willingly offers himself to Xipe Totec."*

The chosen warrior did not require the hands of the priest to help him remain still on the sacrificial slab. He lay down of his own accord, spreading his arms wide to make his chest ready for the knife. Even as the knife plunged he showed no fear, remaining still and alert, staring past the knife and the face of the high priest to the eye of the sun.

As his pulsing heart was held up for the gathered crowds to see there was a collective exhalation of breath that was followed by a great cacophony of drums, flutes, and other musical instruments.

That night there was great feasting for all. Even the poorest inhabitants of the city ate like kings and queens. I could scarce believe the volume of the freshest fruits, slaughtered turkeys, deer, and corn breads that were consumed.

The next morning my father bade our hosts farewell and the caravan set off, minus of course the sacrificed slaves. We made steady progress back to Xaltipan. The return journey being far less arduous than the journey out. Once we had made the summit of the mountains that surrounded the great city it was a steady downhill towards the great sea.

I was idly taking in the views from the heights as the porters strode steadily along the road. Papa seemed to be sleeping and I was paying him no attention as we swayed gently along. There was indeed something soporific about the motion of the palanquin that had at times made me doze off. It was when we stopped for the night that I began to worry. Acalan's beautiful face was pale and covered with glistening beads of sweat.

"My lord, my lord" I called out as I took the risk of touching him by shaking his shoulder. Even a daughter shouldn't initiate physical contact with her lord; had I been a mere commoner, it would have been cause enough to bring about my death. He was slow to respond; finally opening his eyes to gaze at me with eyes that seemed dull and clouded as if one of the mountain mists had entered them. At last he replied:

"Ah Mali, I see that we have reached our resting spot for the night."

"Yes my lord, the servants are lighting the fires and will be preparing our meal"

"Good, let's rest until it is time to eat."

I said nothing but I was very surprised, he was generally a very active man and would ordinarily busy himself instructing his warriors on their dispositions for the night.

When the servants brought the food, we both ate, though Acalan not as heartily as I had come to expect.

The next morning Acalan seemed restored to his normal level of alertness and vigour so I thought no more of his temporary lethargy. We continued our journey. It was the morning of their last day on the road that my dear papa suddenly seemed to take a turn for the worse. Twice the caravan made unscheduled stops while he relieved himself and three or four times, even though he hid himself from view, I could tell he was vomiting. His body was dripping with a strange cold clammy sweat and his strong voice seemed to quaver and lack the strength of lordship.

When we arrived at the great house in Xaltipan, my birth mother took charge of matters at once. Acalan was laid on a bed of feathers and Xoco began immediately to bathe his body with scented waters all the while uttering prayers and incantations. Special herbs were burnt and their smoke directed to pass over his body. She prepared a brew of unknown ingredients that she pressed to his lips. Priests who had been summoned spent the day and night speaking prayers to all the gods.

For three days a dark cloud hung over the house. For three days there was no music, no games, no happy chatter. Even the mice barely dared make a sound as they sought their morsels. When Eleuia and I were permitted to visit him, father seemed barely to recognise us. He already had one foot in another land and this world of ours must be like a shadow to him.

"My dear papa is dying isn't he?" I asked Eli.

"Yes, little one. When he passes he will go to the paradise of Tlalocan where he will live his days in pleasure and the light of the sun. If he had been killed in battle he would have transformed into a hummingbird and followed the daily passage of the sun through the sky"

"So he won't have to go to Mictlan, the underworld?"

"No, his death comes as a result of his journey to the ceremony of Xipe Totec so he will be spared that fate."

I was pleased that my beloved father would be able to spend the remainder of the great cycle in paradise. He was a great and kind lord and deserved an afterlife in paradise.

"Why has he been taken from us?" I asked Eli.

"Not all our work is to be done here on the mortal plane. Perhaps the Gods have some important task for him in other worlds" she replied.

Later I was to realise that it was the way of Gods of all races to give and take as they saw fit without leaving us a note to explain their reasoning.

I wasn't with him when he died, my birth mother Cimatl decreed that only herself, Xoco and two others were allowed to be with him all the time. But I knew. I was helping Eli with the grinding of the maize when I suddenly felt a shadow cross my heart and my breath caught. I looked at Eli, and she just nodded. A moment later we heard the wailing from the house. I ran to Eli and flung my arms around her waist, as Eli gently stroked my hair I could feel tears quietly making their way down my face.

"The priests will take charge now" Eli declared, *"they will cover his body with magic herbs and bind him into a sitting position in preparation for his burial at the temple".*

"Will I be permitted to see him?" I asked.

"Not until the very end when he is taken to the temple for his burial" Eli replied.

For two days I just had to wait and carry on as if nothing had happened. I still ground the corn, I kept up with my weaving and any other task demanded. I would find myself staring blankly into the distance while my inner eye showed me images of my happiest times with papa. These times would never come again.

At last the day of the funeral was upon us. The wrapped body of Acalan was carried by the priests to the temple awash in a continual wave of chanting and music. Eli and I were allowed to follow just behind Cimatl and the priests. At the temple there were more incantations before his body was lowered gently into the burial pit. A red dog was killed. Musical instruments, his best bow, and arrows, his dark green yax tun sword and some of the most precious jewellery was placed into the earth with him. A feast of corn tortilla, roasted deer and every imaginable fruit and vegetable was set to sustain him on his travels. With deep incantations he was covered with red earth and a large, carved, burial stone was laid over his resting place.

For many days after the burial I visited the temple and sat by the stone tracing its lines with my fingers. In the centre of the stone was the face of Huitzilopochtli, god of sun and war, and radiating out from the centre were carved lines that showed the spreading of the sun's rays all over the world.

Father, I have lived a long and eventful life and I must at times pass more quickly over some parts of it lest my time in this life expires before I can finish the story of my journey across this plain; you will forgive me if my narrative jumps at times from one moment in time to another further away.

By the time I had attained my eleventh year my mother had remarried to the lord of a nearby city. Eli and I had no role to play in the marriage ceremony and it now seemed as if I had no status in the life of the city. I didn't mind so much. I busied myself with my domestic duties and continued to be an avid student of every scrap of knowledge I could acquire.

"Eli, how well do you know how to speak Nahuatl the language of the Aztec? I learnt a little while I was in the great city, our lord Acalan translated much of what was going on for me, but I'd like to learn more"

"No, I have not had the opportunity to learn much of that tongue but I will ask Xoco if she is willing to teach you."

"Thank you Eli, I will work hard and make you proud."

Xoco was indeed willing to teach me and agreed to spend a short time each day teaching me; perhaps she felt sorry for my diminished status. Lessons with Xoco were different from learning with Eli. Xoco was very strict and would be very short with me if she thought I wasn't trying hard enough. This rarely happened, in fact I could tell she was impressed at the speed with which I learnt. I only needed to be told the meaning of a word once and I would never forget it.

Cimatl was with child. Her belly began to swell and she spent more and more time in her chambers. Eli and I carried on as usual. More and more we were kept away from the events of the great house, as if they we were deliberately being pushed into the shadows.

One Summer morning I was awoken abruptly by the sounds of singing from the great house. The child had been born. By the tenor of the songs it was clearly alive and well. For a few days I missed out on my Nahuatl lessons, and at last I heard that my birth mother had produced a boy.

I can't remember now how long it was...perhaps three or four cycles of the moon.

I was awoken in the first light of dawn by two of the warriors. They were gentle but firm as they led me into the central courtyard. Waiting there were merchants from Xicalanco, who had brought with them a good selection of woven goods from one of the distant Southern tribes.

Eli had heard the disturbance and rushed out to the courtyard her hair streaming out behind her.

"What is going on here?" she cried out, "what are you doing to the princess?"

"This is none of your concern Eleuia" decreed Cimatl.

I stood there between the two warriors, my eyes wide and roving between the faces of Cimatl and Eli. I knew that my life was to turn in this moment.

"Am I to be sold as a slave?" I asked.

"Clever girl" Cimatl replied, "Now that the gods have granted me a son I have no further use for you."

Eli was crying, her face streaked with tears and her breath coming in ragged gasps. She was about to say something else when I locked my eyes on hers and spoke softly:

"My dearest Eli, say no more. There is nothing we can do and you mustn't put yourself in danger. You have been my friend, my guardian, my teacher, and my mother. I love you."

Eli said no more. She covered her eyes with her forearm and looked away.

I turned away from she who had been my real mother and walked straight up to one of the merchants, holding my hands out in front, ready to be bound.

Chapter three: slavery

My hands were kept bound most of the time, I was connected along with two men to a long pole by fibre ropes that had been tied through holes. The pole could accommodate up to six captives, I wasn't sure if I was pleased or not that our slave pole wasn't full. On the one hand we were more spaced out, on the other the weight of the pole may have been more evenly shared. In the course of my life I've found that many things fall into the twilight between good and bad. I was freed from my bonds to eat and to relieve myself. At night the small group, consisting of the two merchants, a dozen servants and porters, a number of guards, the two male slaves and of course myself, would make camp beside the road. After eating, I would be placed in a wooden cage made from lashed lengths of sturdy wood and left for the night to sleep. The merchants made it very clear to the male servants and porters that I was not to be touched; they were informed that should I no longer be a virgin my value would be greatly diminished. Most likely any man that broke this stricture would be put to death or at the very least have freshly ground hot chillies rubbed onto his genitals.

Our journey wound its way down from the higher lands towards the big sea. The merchants kept me close to them but didn't engage in any conversation; I walked steadily, immersed in my own thoughts, and taking note of the lands I was passing through. I practiced every word of Nahuatl that Xoco had taught me, going over and over the words, mouthing them almost silently until they sounded just the way I had originally heard them. I knew that with this practice, my knowing of the Aztec language would never leave me.

The group stopped at major towns along the way and made trades with some of the goods they carried; woven cloth, statues, carved figures, and cooking implements which were exchanged for items of jewellery and adornment such as gold and silver bracelets and necklaces of jade and turquoise. I wondered at each trading halt if this was to be the place where I would be on-sold and perhaps live out the rest of my life. But clearly the merchants had a plan for me as I was never offered up as part of a negotiation.

After many days the journey took them to the great sea at Coatzacoalcos. For me it was a great wonder to see the great expanse of the sea. It spread out as far as my eyes could reach and was flat and featureless. The blue was a different deeper colour than the blue of the great lakes of the Aztec capitol. It was just as I had dreamt it, but without any great sea serpent! It was hotter down here by the sea, but luckily by the time the sun had climbed to his highest point, a breeze would spring up from the sea to make the heat more tolerable. I liked the smell of the air that wafted in from the sea and I wondered what, if anything, lay on the other side of its blue expanse.

After three passages of the sun they moved us on from Coatzacoalcos. Many days later we reached the much greater city of Comalcalco in the area controlled by the Tabasco alliance. This city, while tiny compared to the majesty of Tenochtitlan, was many times larger than my home in Xaltipan. As the merchant group approached the city we could see a great pyramid and soon we were passing by its base. This was the strangest pyramid I had ever seen; it was made from bricks- not the stone that every other pyramid had been constructed from that I had seen before. At its base was a large and strange statue of a giant toad with wings. The toad had an evil leer on its face and was painted in the brightest red and green, its strange feathered wings were pale blue. I was always interested to learn, and I wished Xoco or someone was there who I could ask about the pyramid and statue. The merchants had bade us not to speak and offered to lash anyone engaging in talk. They reached a building on the edge of the town where they settled down for the night, as usual I was enclosed in my wooden cage.

The next day I alone was taken into the city's central plaza.

There were many merchants assembled there and a number of the nobles of Comalcalco were gathered to examine all the goods up for sale. There were women young and old, and even girls who I guessed to be as young as seven years. This market was apparently solely for the selling of slaves of the female persuasion. Along with the others I was examined to ensure my health. My teeth and skin condition were given special attention. An attendant midwife went along the line of women and girls reaching between their legs. When she reached me our eyes met briefly as I felt her fingers enter my purse and push gently at the barrier they encountered. She nodded; the merchants looked pleased. I stood tall and did not bow my head. I could hear the nobles remarking that I was a handsome looking girl and seemed strong and healthy. Once the sale goods had been examined the merchants and those interested among the nobles retired to one of the houses around the courtyard to negotiate prices and take food.

When at last the nobles emerged it was clear that deals had been done. I was led away by a tall nobleman attended by many servants; this was likely a sign he must be wealthy and of good standing to be accompanied by such a retinue. I was led to a grouping of a dozen modest houses clustered around one substantial one. I was placed into one that clearly served to house both servant and slave women and girls. My bindings were released and I was able to move about freely for the first time since I had left my home.

"What is your name girl?" an older woman asked her.

"I am Malinali of the house of Acalan in Xaltipan" I replied, my head unbowed, my eyes meeting hers.

"That is well and good, but here you are just another slave girl. I am Chiconahui. Here you will be known as Chantico. I will instruct you in the ways of this house. Your life here will be ruled by our lord's will. This is a fair and favourable house. Carry out your duties and you will be well treated. Fail to do so and you will be punished. Try to leave and you will be hunted down and offered as a gift to the sun."

I listened to this stern admonishment in silence. I missed Eli. I missed Acalan. But I was not afraid, a voice inside my head told me that this time would pass and that I wouldn't be a slave forever.

For the most part I found that life was much the same as it had been at home. I soon settled into a daily routine of domestic duties. I cleaned, I cooked, I spun cotton and maguey fibres, I wove, and finally after many days I was called to the lord's chambers to provide him with service.

Entering into the sleeping chamber I was not afraid. I had been told by Eli what happened between men and women in the chamber. This was just another skill I could learn.

"Stand before me girl" he commanded.

"Now remove your robes"

I did as I was instructed, feeling very naked. I could feel the touch of his eyes as they roved all over my body lingering here and there. Then he called me over and began to touch me. He ran his hands over every inch of my body commenting on my beauty and noble bearing as he went. At last he slid his hand between my legs and inserted a finger inside me. He was not forceful, rather his touch was exploratory.

"Good, you are pure" was his only comment.

He took my hand and placed it on his organ. As Eli had shown me, I began to move my hand up and down, moving the loose skin and gradually squeezing as I went. I looked into his eyes with a calm but unafraid stare. I could feel the changes in his organ and heard as his breath came faster and his eyes began to lose their focus.

"Turn around and bend forward" he instructed.

I did as I was told. Despite having been coached for this moment, I let out a little cry as he thrust himself inside me. A moment later he was done. He lay down on his sleeping mat and told me to go. I didn't hurry away. I calmly gathered up my robe. I covered myself. And with the cloth that Eli had advised me to bring, dealt with the blood that was trickling down my legs.

As Eli had told me, the first time was indeed the worst. On subsequent visits to the lord's chambers I was able to relax a little and employ some of the skills that I had learnt but never practiced. Of all the lord's concubines I, Chantico, was for many years the most favoured. While I knew I would never attain the status of a wife, I was treated with deference and not a little jealousy by the other slaves and servants. I stood apart and was not befriended by them. Among the women there was one wizened old crone called Nikte, whose name means flower. This flower was indeed withered, though when I looked at her bones and the skin that now hung loose on her face, I could see that she once may have been a great beauty. Indeed she still held herself with dignity and pride.

"I was once the favoured one of the previous lord" she announced to me one day.

I just nodded but smiled to encourage her to continue.

"I know what it is like, girl, to at once be the favourite, and at the same time to be alone with your privilege."

"Thank you grandmother" I replied, for it seemed a kindness that she was speaking with me with no hint of jealousy or malice. From that day on we became companions. She was my only friend. I would help her with her work when I could, carrying the heavier loads and helping with work that demanded the bending of a back.

I was thirsty for knowledge, it seemed to me that my soul was a parched field ready to soak up any drops of knowledge that fell my way. Whenever I had the opportunity I would seek out Nikte and ask her for stories of the gods and the history of this city. Sometimes she was tired and curt, refusing to speak with me. I persevered and did what little I could to help her with any task she was carrying out. Eventually like the passage of water over stone she was worn down and gave me more and more of her time.

Oh father, please forgive me for digressing. For now I will tell you what I was told of the arrival of the stranger from across the sea who many believed to be the returning God Quetzalcoatl.

Chapter four: The return of Quetzalcoatl

Cortez stood on the poop deck of the Santa Maria de la Concepcion. The wind was at last behind her, and she would surely make better time now. The rest of his fleet were ahead of him and he wanted to be with them as soon as he possibly could.

Antonio, how long until we see land?" He asked his friend and navigator Antonio de Alaminos.

"Not long now, the wind from the stern and the settling of the waves means that we will make good progress" was the reply.

Cortez was anxious to re-unite his fleet, a strong and persistent storm had struck them one day out of Cuba and scattered them. The Santa Maria was the largest of his ships at 100 tons and had fared well enough through the treacherous seas. It was the smaller craft that he was concerned about; it would only be by the grace of God that they would all have survived the mountainous seas that the storm had thrown at them. At Antonio's suggestion, he had instructed all his captains that they were to meet on the island of Cozumel just off the peninsula.

Arriving next day by the first light of dawn, Cortez could see that all his major ships had made it safely into anchorage in the bay. To his dismay, he could also see that five of his smaller brigantines had not made it. Not a good start for his expedition that had cost him all he owned and thrown him into considerable debt to furnish.

Rowing to the beach he was surprised to see that the small native village was deserted and there were signs of destruction- thatched huts that had been burnt and other signs of desecration. He had given all his captains strict instructions that, at least initially, they were to acquire loot by trade not plunder. A brief enquiry soon established that one of his most trusted captains Pedro de Alvarado had led the raid on the village, taking turkeys and other food as well as a small quantity of gold ornaments.

"Pedro, my brother from Estremadura, did you forget my instructions in regard to the treatment of natives?" he enquired. Pedro was a tough and experienced conquistador having already led his own expedition to Yucatán the previous year.

"Yes, but what are we here for if not to lead these heathens to God and avail ourselves of their treasures?" was the cock-sure reply.

"Indeed that is our mission, and to claim these lands for our king. But we will need allies and guides and we must hide our intentions until we have sufficient strength to sweep all before us."

Though patently displeased, Alvarado nodded and bowed his head indicating his acquiescence to his leader's wishes. Cortez ordered that all the stolen goods were to be returned to the villagers and anything that had been already consumed, which included several turkeys that had already met their end on a spit, was to be paid for with the green glass beads that he knew the natives treasured.

By the next day the natives began returning to their village and Cortez instructed his men to assist in the rebuilding of damaged huts. This act of good faith had the hoped for results. Over the next few days all of natives had returned, and through a Spaniard who had been captured by natives on a previous expedition and freed by Cortez's men, Cortez was able to parlay with the chiefs of this and other surrounding villages.

The interpreter, whose name was Jeronimo de Aguilar, was fluent enough in the Maya language which he had taken pains to learn during his two years of captivity.

"Jeronimo, tell these chieftains that tomorrow there will be a great display here on the beach for their interest." Cortez *instructed.*

When Aguilar had conveyed this to the assembled crowd, Cortez continued:

"Ask them to send runners to any nearby villages or towns inviting their leaders to participate."

Turning to Pedro and the other captains he said:

"I want to put on a show of our weaponry and fighting skill that will be heard far and wide. Fear is one of the greatest weapons of any victor and I want future opponents to begin to doubt themselves."

The next day Cortez and his men indeed put on quite a show.

First thing in the morning the horses were unloaded from the ships. Sturdy leather straps were wrapped under their bellies front and back, and by means of the ship-board cranes they were lowered into smaller craft to be ferried to the shore. A collective gasp of amazement rose up from the crowd. Never in their lives had the native people seen such creatures. Their amazement only grew when Cortez' men shining in their steel breastplates and helmets were mounted on the horses. Cortez ordered the cavalrymen to race up and down the beach waving their swords and crying out their battle cry: *"For God and St. James!"*

Following this impressive cavalry display, the rest of his 500 or so men displayed their wares. Pikemen lined up in an orderly line, their sharpened pikes forming a glinting steel fence. Crossbowmen sent flights of bolts whistling through the air. And finally the harquebusiers and small cannon unleashed a roar of noise and a cloud of acrid smoke that had some of the natives running for cover.

Now that he had displayed his little army's military potential, Cortez felt emboldened to take a step that he thought necessary in his role as an agent of God. Not far from the beach, where they had set their camp, there was a small temple set upon a hill that overlooked the sweep of the bay. Cortez had been horrified to hear stories that sacrifices both human and animal were undertaken at the temple. His scouts had also reported that there were many idols and images of strange gods set about. He accompanied fifty or so of his men to the temple. Arriving there they were shocked to see human bones and the smears of blood and entrails across a sacrificial altar. The soldiers set to work smashing the statues with cudgels and throwing the pieces down the hillside. The altar was scrubbed with lime and water to remove as much of the stain as possible. He instructed his men to cut some branches and fashion a cross to be erected at the head of the altar and asked his priest Bartolome de Olmedo to consecrate the site in the name of the virgin Mary.

After several weeks gathering more stores and trading the much-prized green glass beads with the natives, he was ready to set off for the mainland. After many days at sea but fortunately propelled by favourable winds they arrived at the mouth of what they later named the Tabasco river. This was to be the launching point of their journey into the mysterious heartland of this exotic land.

Chapter five: A new master

Rumours ran through the city like rivulets of water after a heavy rainfall.

"Strangers have arrived from the East!"

"Quetzalcoatl has returned!"

"The strangers have white skins and hair on their faces!"

"They sit on giant creatures and shine like the sun!"

"Thunder and smoke follow them around!"

I heard all these rumours, and more, as I went about my daily chores. Chiconahui had come to trust me. I rather like to think that she saw me for who I was. Due to her importance in the workings of the city, Chiconahui heard much more of what was really going on and undertook to update me as she could.

"It is true Chantico that strangers have arrived. A runner came to the lord just today to tell him of the events down at the river mouth. He described the strangers arriving in giant canoes with huge white cloths hung from trees that sprout from their surface. And the stories about giant creatures and shining silver coats are all true it seems."

"What do you think is going to happen?" I asked.

"The lord has gathered his warriors and is journeying to the river mouth as have all the other notables. I think there is a good chance that there will be war" was the disturbing reply that I received.

For many passages of the sun rumours continued to buzz around like a disturbed bee swarm.

At last, one of the lord's men arrived back from the coast and all the people were gathered around to hear the story:

"All the cities and towns of Tabasco had sent warriors and in total we numbered many thousands. Our chieftains ordered the strangers to leave our lands but they refused and many small battles followed. In the end at Centla there was a major battle. Our warriors rushed at them in a huge wave as if they were the very ocean. Drums were beating and the conch shells were blown to create a great and terrifying noise. As our flood of warriors neared the strangers there was a huge noise and great clouds of smoke. Warriors began to fall as if smote by invisible arrows and then the great beasts with men atop charged at us. The strangers hacked at us with their silver swords and their silver cloaks protected them from our arrows and darts. The great beasts trampled on the living, the dying, and the dead alike. The ground was covered in the blood of our people and the air was rent with their screams and cries. In the end those of us with still beating hearts ran for our very lives."

"And our lord?" Chiconahui asked.

"He is injured, with a cut across his chest but will be alright, he is returning on his litter. He sent me on ahead" he replied.

The following day the lord arrived and was closeted in the great house. He was attended by priests and shaman who would seek to heal his wounds.

Several days later I was again awoken by warriors standing over my sleeping mat. Chiconahui was with them.

"What is this?" I asked her.

"To make peace with the strangers our lord is offering gifts. You are to be one of those gifts."

I looked at Chiconahui and my gaze was steady.

"So be it" I said, offering my wrists to the warriors to be bound.

"No!" interjected Chiconahui, *"there is no need to bind her, she understands the will of the gods."*

More the will of men than the gods I thought but kept silent.

Every noble house in Tabasco had contributed gifts that were to be offered to these fearsome strangers. As well as me, the lord had offered three other slave girls and other goods of value. In total the Tabascans had gathered twenty slave girls, a horde of jewellery, golden cups, and many items of food. This haul of booty was taken down to the coast for presentation to the strangers.

My first sight of the strangers filled me with wonder. The stories were indeed true. These were warriors like no other. They held strange weapons quite unlike the jade or obsidian swords, lances, bows, and dart throwers used by Tabascan and Mexica alike. The shining silver coats, that I had been told of, were clearly armour but very different from the thick cotton padding that my people or the Mexica used. Many of these strange warriors sat atop huge creatures many times larger than the largest deer. These creatures would at times paw at the earth and snort noisily. I could see why these creatures had wreaked such havoc among all the warriors they had confronted.

There was a conversation between the leader of these newcomers and the chiefs. One of their kind could speak Maya and was acting as an interpreter and I could catch fragments of the conversation. It seemed the leader of the strangers was willing to accept the gifts and make peace.

All the girls and women who were to be gifted to the strangers received instruction to walk forward in a line. I was in the middle of the line and watched as my predecessors as they went through an unusual ceremony. A black robed man approached them and began intoning words in a foreign language. The interpreter was doing his best to translate this language into Maya but seemed to be struggling with it. Water was being splashed onto the slaves as they one by one went to the black robed man. They were forced to kneel and the water was liberally splashed over their heads while the man-made a cross sign over their bodies and on their foreheads.

When it was my turn I knelt straight away and this seemed to please the strangers. The leader of the ceremony began intoning his words and the translator busied himself keeping up:

"Father, you give us grace through your sacramental signs,

Which tells us of the wonders of your unseen power.

In Baptism we use your gift of water,

Which you have made a rich symbol

Of the grace you give us in this sacrament."

I could well appreciate the importance of water, along with the sun, water was essential to life.

"At the very dawn of creation

Your spirit breathed on the waters,

Making them the wellspring of all holiness."

As the water was being sprinkled on my head I heard the interpreter's words:

"Dona Marina, I baptise you in the name of the Father, and of the Son, and of the Holy Spirit."

By this I gathered that I had acquired yet another name, and henceforth was to be called Marina. I was instructed to stand and *"go forth with God"*.

I was given to one of the leaders of this warlike people, a man with the overly long name of Alonso Hernandez Puertocarrero. This man was short and stocky, with bad skin covered in pits and pimples. He was not cruel to me. I came to hate the foul smell of his breath; it was just like that of one of the war-dogs that the strangers had brought with them. In the subsequent days I found that very little had changed in my life. I was grinding maize, making tortilla, preparing food, and serving it, very much as I had done for all of my young life. When Alonso took me to his bed it was quick. His organ spurted forth almost before he pushed inside me. Then he would roll over and emit thunderous snores that shook the rafters of the little house where we spent our nights.

The only difference for me was the ones I served. These strangers, Spaniards as I now knew them to be called, were in the end no different from other men. They were no crueller or kinder than all other men. In their religious beliefs they indeed differed. They did not worship the sun. Despite their prowess and savagery in battle, they talked with abhorrence about what they had seen of the sacrifices made to ensure the rising of the sun each morning.

I was curious about the Spaniard who had done all the translating for the Spanish leader.

"How is it that you know our language Señor Aguilar?" I asked, speaking in Maya but using the correct Spanish form of address that I had already learnt.

"Due to my misfortune and my fortune Dona Marina" he replied.

"How so?" I asked.

"I was on a ship that hit a shoal near the coast of an island called Jamaica. The ship foundered and I and 19 compatriots were able to escape its fate in a small boat. We only had one set of oars and though we took it in turns to heave away, we could make little progress against the wind and currents. Soon the harsh wind had blown us far out into the sea. We had no food or water or shelter from the sun. One by one compatriots began to die. Some in their fevered desperation took to drinking the salt water of the sea. Others such as myself drank our own urine. When we at last hit land there were just nine of us left alive, and barely so at that."

I was gripped by this tale of desperation and urged Aguilar to continue.

"We were taken captive by the local tribe at our landing place. Our leader the conquistador Valdivia and three others were killed at once, cooked and eaten in some heathen ceremony. The rest of us were placed in wooden cages to await an unknown fate. We were fed well and given water. It dawned on us that we were being fattened like pigs for a future sacrifice. In desperation we worked together to secretly loosen the wooden stakes that formed our cages and one moonless night we were able to free ourselves and escape. In the darkness of the jungle I became separated from my comrades and journeyed on alone not knowing where I was going. In the end I was captured by another tribe and enslaved."

Tears were rolling down Aguilar's face as he recounted this dire tale. I reached my hand out to his and asked: *"How did you sustain yourself through such a gruelling experience?"*

At this he reached into his robe and pulled out a torn and tattered object. *"This is my book of prayers, I managed to keep it with me the whole time of my captivity. By sending my prayers every day up to Our Lord I believe I was given the strength and good fortune to survive."*

"And what became of your comrades?" I asked.

"I do not know what fate befell all but one. My friend Guerrero won his freedom from the tribe who had captured him. He became a respected warrior and leader among them, adopting the tattoos and markings of the tribe, even going as far as having a piece of jade inserted into his lip. He took a chief's daughter as his wife and she bore him a daughter and two sons. I was allowed to visit with him but when I asked him if he longed for freedom and a return to Cuba he declared that he was happy with his new life and had no wish to return to his old ways."

"So how long in all were you a captive Señor Aguilar?"

"Eight long years."

I was impressed by this story. I could certainly relate to going from one servitude to another. This man had been able to sustain himself through the power of his faith through eight long years!

I took every opportunity I could find to listen in when Aguilar was translating from Spanish into Maya. The Spaniards had many meetings with the Tabascan chiefs who continued to ply them with gifts. They were particularly interested in the items of gold that they were gifted. Through Aguilar the Spanish leader continually asked:

"Do you have more gold? Where does the gold come from? Are there mines hereabouts?"

The Tabascans replied that no, they had no more gold but that the Aztec had much more and so saying they pointed to the North West.

When I finally lay down to sleep at night, as well as the Christian prayers I had been instructed to say, I went over and over the new Spanish words I had heard.

As I went about my duties, which were no different than they had been for my whole life, I carefully watched the strangers. I liked to go and watch the horses, they were skittish when I first approached them, but soon became used to my look and smell. The young boys who were tasked with looking after the animals were happy enough for me to approach them and even touch their quivering flanks. It was strange to me that these giant animals could be so gentle, and yet their purpose was to aid the Spaniards in striking terror into their enemy's hearts. I wondered at the gentleness in their great liquid eyes and could only suppose that it was their dedication to the soldiers that led them to be able to engage in battle.

Despite their strange equipment, these Spaniards were definitely men not gods. They behaved more or less the same as warriors from my home or the Tabascan warriors. Much of their time was spent lounging around and playing games that I had yet to understand. At night they would drink the dark red wine that they cherished and become rowdy with joking and singing songs, some of which I later learnt were very ribald.

I paid particular attention to their leader, Señor Cortes, he looked quite different from Acalan or other chiefs and kings I had met. He was tall and seemed to be quite muscular; his hair dark and to shoulder length, and as with many of these so-called Spaniards he had hair on his face. I thought his slightly grey skin colour to be his least attractive feature though somewhat redeemed by his twinkling dark eyes. He seemed to be well respected by his men and though at first I couldn't understand what was said I could tell that he was used to issuing commands and being obeyed. I often observed him joking and having fun with all his men, even the common soldiers and not just the captains. I was determined to learn their language and spent every minute of every day listening with a keen ear.

After many days, during which Cortes ordered his men to work on repairs to their strange boats and to sharpen swords, lances, and other weapons I didn't recognise, the soldiers their slaves and servants began to load the boats.

I had only ever been in a canoe and found these huge boats fascinating. They were as big as a very grand house, and the biggest of them could hold many score of men and several horses. It took all of two days to load these sea-going houses.

When all was ready, vast white cloths were hauled up the tree trunks and the ship got underway. I was put into a cramped space in the boat along with all the other slaves. Not all of these slaves were Tabascan, I found out that some had been brought with the Spaniards from the island of Cuba. Of all the trials of my life I found being confined in this dark wooden space, the air fetid, and the smells of animals and people mingling into a foul brew, most horrid. I found myself just longing to be standing outside with a fresh breeze blowing my hair and filling my lungs. It was hard to even be absolutely certain about the passage of the sun. Maybe the necessary sacrifices had been neglected and the sun had not risen. Whenever the door to the space was opened, I would approach the ladder just to see if the sun was in the sky or not. I could judge that the waves on the sea must be small as the ship only rocked gently from side to side.

After what I thought might be three days I could hear a commotion up on the deck of the boat. Clearly they had arrived at their destination, I heard the sounds of shouted orders, and finally my fellow slaves and I were released from our dark captivity. Up on the deck of the ship at last, breathing air that had never tasted so sweet, blinking in the unaccustomed brightness of the day, I could see that we were in another wide bay.

From the shore two large dugout pirogues were paddling towards the Santa Maria. Each held a number of finely dressed chiefs and priests. I knew straight away that these were Aztec- their clothing and manner was familiar from my trip to the city of the lakes with my father. Memory is like an unexpected cloudburst. Unbidden thoughts, images, sounds, and smells from the past fall on us and we can but wait for them to wash over us. Seeing the Aztec, I was awash with memories of my journey to the city of the lakes with my father. A soft sadness filled my heart. I missed him. I missed the life I had enjoyed with him; my life had changed forever when he passed to the next world.

Cortes motioned to these finely robed emissaries to come aboard using a rope ladder that had been lowered. When the delegation were all assembled on the deck began to quietly talk in Nahuatl with one of the porters who had carried the gifts on board. He told me that the great Aztec lord Montezuma had heard about the arrival of the strangers. Rumours said that Montezuma had consulted the gods for many days but still hadn't determined if they were friend or foe.

Cortes called to Aguilar to come forth and translate so that he could parlay with them. The Mexica had brought fine gifts with them, including many more gold items than the Spaniards had seen before.

"Señor Aguilar, bid our guests welcome and let them know that we have come with peaceful intentions and that we only wish to trade and spread the word of God."

"My captain, these are Aztec from the great city of Tenochtitlan by the great inland lakes, they speak only Nahuatl, a tongue I have not learnt."

Cortes hid his annoyance. He knew from the experience of earlier conquistadors that communication was the key to any dealings with the natives. He was gently stroking his beard when he noticed me deep in conversation with a porter as I tapped him for information about the great city.

"Aguilar, bring me that slave girl" he commanded.

I was brought to him, and for the first time I could see him paying attention to me. I stood proudly, my back straight, my eyes clear as he gazed on me.

"Aguilar, does this girl know the language of our guests?"

"Yes Señor Cortes, she is fluent in that language" he responded.

"And you can talk to her in her own language?

"That is so senor" he replied.

"Well, she will work with you to translate our words, it will be cumbersome, but we need to make ourselves understood and likewise be comprehended. I fear that a false step now could rain calamities down on our heads."

It was slow. When the Aztec spoke, I translated into Maya, and then Aguilar would translate into Spanish, and then the whole process was reversed so that Cortes could be understood. It was a clumsy but effective enough process. Gold trinkets, feathered vests, cotton goods and other fine gifts were given to the Spaniards. In exchange the Aztec were given some iron tools, casks of wine and glass beads. Cortes made it clear that he intended to land his force and that his presence ashore was not open for negotiation.

Soon the smaller boats were swarming around the bigger boats ferrying cargo, men, and horses ashore. I was separated from the other slaves, and went in one of the boats with Cortes, Aguilar, and some of the other leaders of the Spanish. From then on I was to be treated differently from the other slaves and was kept close to Cortes at all times.

Two days later a messenger arrived with important news that Aguilar and I translated:

"Tendile, an important governor will be arriving soon. He comes at the instruction of the great lord Montezuma to parlay with you and offer you gifts of great value."

"Tell this messenger to return to this Tendile and convey our great pleasure to receive him."

Just as Aguilar was about to translate this into Maya I stepped forward and translated it directly from the Spanish. Cortes looked at Aguilar who just shrugged. Perhaps realising that he was no longer indispensable.

When the messenger had departed to run back to the Aztec delegation Cortes turned back to me:

"Dona Marina it seems you have learnt my language"

"Yes my lord the gods gave me the ear and tongue to master speech easily" I replied.

As a test of my fluency in Spanish he then asked:

"Tell me then about these Mexica and the city they come from."

"The Mexica came down from the North many hundreds of seasons ago. When they arrived at the great lakes they saw a huge eagle perched on a cactus, devouring a snake. They knew this to be an omen that the place was to be their new home. They are the most fearsome of all warriors but also clever at forming alliances. They have allied themselves with the people of Texcoco and Tlacopan; they have defeated all the other cities including my own and taken tributes from far and wide."

"Have you seen their city?" Cortes asked.

"I visited once with my father Acalan sir" I replied.

"Tell me what it was like and what the warriors were like" he commanded.

"The city is almost beyond description. It sits on a vast mirror-like lake and you can only access it along broad causeways that ten men can stand abreast on. Below these causeways there are dozens of canoes paddling by, carrying goods and people. The buildings are huge, they tower up into the sky. There are temples everywhere."

"And the people?"

"The people are too many to count and there are many warriors and priests who attend to the ruler Montezuma."

"One final question" Cortes asked: *"Do they practice human sacrifice?"*

"Yes, I was in the city for twenty passages of the sun, every day at least a dozen slaves were sacrificed. There are sacrifices every day otherwise the sun won't rise."

The next day Cortes ordered that a mass be said to honour that it was Good Friday. I had spent many hours talking with the priests, especially Fray Bartolome de Olmedo who seemed to be the most senior of the priests. I found it interesting that the Spaniards talked about having only one God but made shrines to Mary and talked about 'the Holy Spirit' as well. The stories Bartolome told me about Jesus and the miracles he had accomplished were intriguing. This Christ certainly seemed like one of the least war-like Gods I had ever heard of. But these were clearly war-like soldiers who showed no qualms at slaughtering their enemies in hundreds.

The mass was held on the beach. It was nearing the middle of the day. I felt sorry for the Spanish soldiers in their heavy metal armour and helmets as they knelt under the blazing sun. I could see the insects biting them, and their ineffective efforts to swat them away as sweat ran freely down their necks and faces. I was to become well used to attending mass. This ceremony was held every seventh day at least and more often at certain times.

The next day I asked Fray Bartolome:

"Why did your lord Jesus not gather up his followers and fight against the Roman overlords?"

"Jesus led by example and preaching. He set an example that was based on his teachings that were all about love. Followers were taught to love God and love one another. If injured they were implored to turn the other cheek- meaning not to strike back."

"But Senor Cortes and the others are such fierce warriors! I don't see them turning the other cheek!" I retorted.

"Ah but they are here to save the souls of these heathen. All the unconverted will spend all eternity in the fires of hell. The soldiers will only fight those who attack them or refuse to allow their souls to be saved."

I listened to this and pondered the differences between the beliefs of my birth and the beliefs of these strangers; I thought that they truly came from a different world.

On Easter Sunday, in the year of our lord 1519, as I had learnt to know it, Tendile, an ambassador sent by the Aztec emperor Montezuma arrived. Tendile was a tall man with an aquiline nose set in a broad face, he bore himself with great dignity. His was accompanied by a vast contingent, perhaps several thousand, of richly dressed attendants and slaves. They spread out behind him like a sea of brightly coloured feathers, dressed in the finest robes and jewels.

"Dona Marina, welcome our guests and bade them wait while we celebrate another mass in honour of Our Lord's resurrection."

I dutifully instructed the ambassador that in honour of their arrival there would be a religious ceremony to the God that these strangers worshipped. The Aztec patiently waited while Fray Bartolome conducted yet another mass. Then Tendile stepped forward, wet his fingers with his own saliva, and bent to the earth to coat his fingers in soil which he then touched to his own lips.

"What is he doing?" Cortes asked.

"He is showing his respect and love for the land on which we stand" I replied.

Through me, Tendile spoke to Cortes:

"I bring you greetings from the most high and mighty Montezuma, lord of all Aztec, leader of the triple alliance, and guardian of the sacred truths. He wishes to let you know that you are welcome to stay in this place but must not, without his permission, venture further into the interior".

So saying he motioned to his followers who brought forward many chests full of the most brightly coloured feather work, gold items and jewellery.

In exchange Cortes ordered his men to present Tendile with a red cap embroidered with an image of Saint George slaying the dragon and a heavy, carved wooden Spanish armchair.

Tendile was intrigued by the Spanish helmets that shone in the bright light, their curved sides and top catching the sun and glinting with captured sunbeams. He asked if he could examine one and was duly presented with one by Cortes. He could see the way that the Spanish men seemed to prize the golden objects above all others and asked me to enquire:

"You and your followers seem to prize gold more than Quetzal feathers, jewels or anything else, why is that?"

"My men and I suffer from an affliction of the heart that can only be cured by gold; without gold we would die before our time" was Cortes' translated reply.

"I wish to meet with your Montezuma that we may exchange more gifts and learn each other's ways" Cortes instructed me to tell Tendile.

"You have barely just heard of our prince and yet you now demand to meet him!" was the sharp retort that I relayed from Tendile.

Cortes asked me to mollify the ambassador with promises that, for now, the Spanish forces would remain glued to the coast. He got me to stress however that he too served a great ruler and that there was a regal expectation that Cortes, on behalf of his own lord, would deal directly with Montezuma at some point. To complete this day of trading gifts and negotiating Cortes decided on yet another display of his military prowess.

As they had done on the beach of Cozumel the Spaniards set about putting on a great show to impress the Mexica with their horses, their slathering war-dogs, their crossbowmen, and most of all with their cannon and musketry fire.

That evening the Spanish captains sat with Cortes around a fire drinking good Spanish wine from some of the gold and silver cups that they had been gifted. I was invited to join them and with some hesitancy I did so. I could feel the eyes of these men devouring every inch of my body with their eyes. Cortes bade me sit beside him, and by this I came to feel that I was of such value to him that I would be under his protection and was not to be bothered by the other men. That evening I fully expected to be instructed to join him in his bed but to my surprise he merely bade me good evening and I was allowed to retire to my own sleeping space. As I lay down to sleep I wondered if perhaps my form did not please this great warrior.

The following day Tendile departed, promising to return with more messages and gifts from Montezuma. As a farewell gift he presented Cortes with two thousand additional slaves.

"I am amazed at the generosity of this ambassador of Montezuma, why do you think he is being so generous?" Cortes asked me when the last of the Aztec were gone.

"The Aztec are very rich; they receive tribute from many cities. They will be wanting to impress you with their wealth and power. Also, perhaps they have heard of your men and their fighting prowess, the display you showed them on the beach will have added to that impression, so perhaps they are just a little afraid. I must tell you lord that there is a legend regarding the return of Quetzalcoatl from the East. Before I met you myself, I too believed that you might not be a man but rather Quetzalcoatl" I replied.

"Who is this Quetzalcoatl?"

"He is one of the great creators. He could take many forms appearing as he wished in all manner of forms though most often as a feathered serpent. He brought rain to the fields and fertility to all the people. He grants both death and resurrection to the worthy. He is the god of war but also the patron of priests, the lord of goldsmiths and master of the calendar."

"You have spoken of him in the past tense, is he now dead?" Cortes asked.

"It is not known sir. His brother Tezcatlipoca performed acts of black magic to banish him across the great eastern sea. Legend says that one day he may return to take his rightful place among the gods."

"Thank you Dona Marina, that is useful information, it may be greatly to my advantage to appear as if I were this Quetzalcoatl!"

Over the next months Tendile returned on further visits, each time bearing rich loads of gifts but re-iterating that the strangers should stay at the coast and not venture inland.

Meanwhile, I had been noticing that the Spaniards and their servants were suffering greatly from the conditions on this part of the coast. Finally I approached him with my concerns:

"My lord, this part of the coast that you have chosen is not a good location for your base. The dunes are too hot in the heat of the day and the swamps nearby are unhealthy. The swarms of biting insects that so terrorise your men are worse here than elsewhere. The water here is not so good to drink and there are few deer or turkeys to hunt."

It seemed that my words confirmed what he had been thinking. Around a dozen of his men had succumbed to infected wounds from earlier fighting, but more had died from a mysterious fever affliction. Spurred by my proffered advice he sent a scouting expedition in two of his ships to find a more salubrious location for his base. When the ships returned they reported that around forty miles up the coast they had found a better landing spot with clean running waters, plenty of game, and most importantly much less insect life. He quickly made up his mind to re-locate the camp. Most of his men were to take the ships North to the new location while he and about a hundred would journey on land.

"Dona Marina, do you wish to travel on my ships or with me along the coast?" he asked me. My last experience on one of the great ships had been most unpleasant, so despite my new status I was in no hurry to have a repeat voyage.

"My wish is to stay with you my lord, and if it be your will, to ride on one of your horses" I replied.

The next day I had my first riding lesson given to me by Cortes himself. As he assisted me to mount one of the smaller horses he said: *"Dona Marina, you show more courage and wisdom than I any noblewoman that I ever met back home in Medellin!".*

Handing me the reins his eyes met mine and I was taken by the strength of his gaze that seemed to penetrate my soul and yet carried great warmth. The horse he had chosen for me was a fairly docile creature called Isabella; within a couple of days Isabella and I were firm friends and I had mastered the art of riding her. Meanwhile, the ship-borne part of his army were loaded onto the ships and set sail to the North leaving the bay they had named San Juan de Ulua behind.

The journey up the coast was uneventful. As we rode alongside each other Cortes and I told each other of our birth-places and earlier lives. In this way I learnt that his family while by no means poor had been only minor hidalgo, and that as a young man he yearned for adventures in the New World that were not available in Spain. For his part Cortes expressed surprised to discover that I had once been a princess of high birth before being sold into slavery.

On arrival at the new location for their base I found that the ships were already partially unloaded. With his usual energy and authority, Cortes set about laying out a plan for a town that his now numerous slaves were to construct. He was determined to ensure that every act that he undertook was to be done in the name of the king, not the governor of Cuba with whom he had clashed many times. To this end he had documents drawn up by Fray Bartolome claiming this area in the name of King Charles the Fifth and naming the town he was constructing as Villa Rica de la Vera Cruz.

Several weeks later his scouts came upon a group of natives who had clearly been watching developments. He ordered his cavalry to bring these people to him so that he might question them about the area. These natives looked unlike any other people I had ever seen. Their ears and noses had huge holes where big pieces of obsidian or jade stone had been inserted. Their lips were cut in the middle to permanently reveal their blackened teeth. To both our eyes they looked stranger than anyone we had so far encountered.

"Dona Marina, please ask them who they are and where their town or city is".

I tried addressing them in Maya but soon enough I discovered that they spoke a totally different language. I tried Nahuatl and discovered that some of them spoke enough Nahuatl for me to communicate with them.

"These people are Totonacs and their town is called Cempoala. They say they have been watching us since we arrived in the bay. They have issued an invitation for us to journey to their town and meet with their chief" I told him. *"But I'm not sure they are to be trusted lord, if you go, take a strong force"* I added.

I was pleased that he was willing to accept my counsel. He assembled a strong contingent of cavalry, crossbowmen, harquebusiers, and pikeman.

"You must come with us Marina; I can't do this without you" he told me.

I was very pleased. He now considered my assistance essential, and I noticed that he had dropped the formality of calling me Dona. Even though I was probably still a slave it had really began to feel that I was equal with this strange fierce man from across the ocean.

The expedition to Cempoala confirmed for Cortes that they had picked a much better site for the new town. As they marched under the shade of many palm trees, their passage startled great numbers of deer and turkeys indicating that there were plenty to be hunted. Arriving within view of the town it seemed at first that the temples of the town were made of pure silver, they shone so brightly in the sunlight. Envoys of the chief met them and led them through the streets of the town to a central square. The houses were brightly painted in blue, green, yellow and red. The temples and as it turned out multiple pyramids were not made of silver but were bright with fresh lime-wash that must have created the illusion of silver from afar.

Cortes and his warriors were impressed by the buildings in this town. Everything was in good order and gardens and buildings were all being kept tidy and cared for. Through me, Cortes asked if he and a small contingent could be permitted to explore the town. This was duly granted by a finely dressed man who told me that the chief of the town would be arriving soon. Cortes took a dozen of his most experienced swordsmen to examine the major buildings of the town, he granted me permission to walk by his side but instructed me to keep close at all times.

Climbing the steps to the temple perched atop the highest of the pyramids we entered through an archway. The sight that greeted us was horrifying. Though I had witnessed many sacrifices from afar I was not inured to their impact. The corpses of a dozen young boys lay piled in one corner of the space. Their blood was still gathering in dark puddles on the ground. Flies were already busy feasting, crawling all over the faces and sipping at the blood that lay congealing all around. Each body had been deprived of its limbs which were in another pile nearby. Arrayed on silver plates, that were lined along an altar, were their hearts: still warm, but already attracting the attention of a black swarm of flies.

"My God what is this?" cried Cortes turning to me.

"It is a sacrifice to ensure the rising of the sun and the well-being of the people" I replied calmly.

"It is the work of the devil" was his curt response.

Walking back down to the plaza we could see that the square had filled up with natives of the city curious to see the Spaniards. The Totonac chief had arrived on a litter borne by eight strong warriors. He was an immense man. His belly was bigger than that of three ordinary men and thick folds of fat flowed like lava down from his body onto the litter. He began to speak in loud tones pointing and gesticulating wildly. When he was done Cortes turned to me for translation.

"His name is Tlacochcalcatl. His people were defeated by the Aztec only three years ago. Since then they have been forced to pay tribute to Montezuma. This tribute has become more onerous every time the Aztec tax collectors arrive. Many dozens of their young men and women are demanded as slaves and sacrifices, and the richest of their hand-crafts and jewels are taken. He wonders if, given your defeat of the Tabascans, you would be willing to help his people throw off the yoke of Mexica oppression."

When I had finished the translation I added:

"My lord, these people are strong warriors. Montezuma and his allies are great in numbers. If you end up fighting the Aztec you will need many allies yourself, despite your army's prowess."

"Ask him how many warriors he and his people can field in battle" Cortes instructed.

I duly translated the question and answer.

"He says that if all the Totonacs join him they have more than a hundred thousand warriors in all. There is one tribe, the Tlaxcala, who are still fighting the Aztec and have not yet been fully defeated who will be another powerful ally."

"My god am I selling my soul to the devil if I ally with these murderous fiends?" He cried out, as much I thought for the benefit of his men as for me.

"The practice of sacrifice is everywhere in these lands my lord, if you are defeated by Montezuma through lack of forces then all your enterprise is for nought" I responded.

His look told me that he had not expected such strategic judgement from a woman, let alone a native woman. The time would come when he was no longer surprised and would trust my judgement in these matters implicitly. He paused, then nodded his assent and sought my assistance to hammer out a treaty with Tlacochcalcatl. This agreement was to be the template for more to come.

That evening Cortes invited me to join a meeting of his captains. He asked me to give his key men a description of this empire that they were soon to venture into. I did my best to describe what I knew of the empire, prefacing my remarks with the fact that I had been a mere child of eight years at the time of my visit. They were particularly interested in what I remembered of the capital Tenochtitlan and at his urging I did my best to describe the gold and other riches I had seen as a child. The men were curious but also restless as I told my tale it seemed to me that many of his captains were doubting the value of this venture. Cortes had already sent most of the gold and gifts they had acquired back to Spain on one of the ships. Despite his explanation that by keeping in favour with King Charles they would secure the right to take much of the vast wealth within for themselves: these were not happy men.

Cortes was determined to find a suitable site to build a fort from which he could dominate the surrounding countryside. It was while engaged in a scouting expedition to locate the most suitable site that news came of Aztec tax collectors having arrived in one of the nearby towns to collect their dues in goods and slaves. Cortes was keen to continue to negotiate with the Aztec, he had already discussed his desire to journey to Tenochtitlan with me. He took me aside into one of the newly constructed houses and for the first time directly sought my counsel as to how best to deal with these tax collectors.

"On the one hand I have promised my new Totonac allies to support them to throw off the Aztec yoke. On the other hand, from what you have told me we have not yet got the strength to win an all-out war with the Aztec so it would seem wise not to provoke their enmity too soon."

I paused before answering, sensing that this was a pivotal moment in the journey of my life.

"Have your Totonac allies capture the tax collectors and bring them to you; tell them you only want the noblemen who are the actual tax collectors and to allow their attendants and slaves to escape into the jungle. Then have the collectors brought to you as your prisoners. You must speak with these important Aztec and then release them to go scurrying back to Montezuma speaking of your largesse."

"A cunning plan indeed Marina! But not without risk." He went on: *"This will certainly curry favour with Montezuma. But what of my new Totonac allies? Will they not feel betrayed if I release the prisoners?"* He asked.

"Only if they discover the truth my lord. You can say that one of your guards failed to secure them properly for the night and for this he has been severely punished."

He looked at me then with a smile that was entirely different from those that normally spread across his face.

He wasted no time putting this plan into effect, adding for the Totonac chief's benefit that from this day forward the Totonac need never again pay tribute to the Aztec. The two high born Aztec who were in charge of tax collection were duly brought to kneel at his feet. Their necks were yoked together and they seethed with umbrage. Cortes dismissed the Totonac warriors who had brought them and asked me to speak with the prisoners.

I conveyed to him that these men were filled with outrage at this treatment by the Totonac, and that their attendants who had escaped would be reporting this to their great lord Montezuma, who would send one of his generals with a great force to avenge this indignity. Cortes went right up to these finely dressed men who held their heads high in haughty disdain despite their current circumstance.

He instructed me to address them:

"My lords please accept my deepest and sincerest apologies for the way you have been treated. I had asked my Totonac friends to offer you food and drink and treat you in the manner to which you are accustomed. There is no doubt that either I was misunderstood or one of their leaders has acted without sanction. Either way be assured that I will deal with this outrage in a swift and firm manner."

He ordered that the men be released and immediately be offered food and wine. When he sensed that their ruffled feathers had been sufficiently calmed, he presented them with a fine sword and an intricately carved wooden box. The noblemen were especially impressed with the sword, a finely wrought instrument of death made of the finest steel from a city in his homeland called Toledo, its hilt crusted with jewels and finely etched designs.

When the Aztec were well fed, and perhaps a little tipsy on good Valencian wine, he bade me tell them:

"Please return to your great lord with these gifts and once again assure him that we mean him and his great empire no ill. I am keen to meet with him face to face, as I have been instructed to do, by my great King Charles who lives far away across the ocean."

The Aztec nobles agreed to convey this message to Montezuma and went on their way with this message of goodwill and the gifts that had pleased them so well.

I was well pleased that night when Cortes turned to me and thanked me for coming up with this cunning stratagem. I smiled, but then I hesitated. I have never been one to turn away from what needs to be done so I asked him:

"Senor, I am your slave yet you have never ordered me to your bedroom at night. Why is that so? Do I not please you?"

Now it was his turn to hesitate, and I wondered if I had over-stepped my mark and offended him. I could count my heartbeats as I waited. Finally he replied: *"Yes you are my slave Marina. But you are unlike any slave I have been given before. To me you are more noble and more capable than any woman I have ever met, even those at home in Medellin. I give you your freedom, and in that freedom you may choose to come to my bed or not."*

I stood very still. My breath fluttered in my chest like a captured butterfly. I replied at last: *"Thank you my lord, you honour me."*

Cortes laughed and smiling at me replied: *"There is to be no more 'my lord'. From now on if we are alone together it is just Hernan, when we are with my men Senor Cortes will do."*

Now it was my turn to smile as I turned away whispering: *"Thank you and goodnight Hernan."*

Chapter six: A free woman

I realised that for the first time since I was a child I was free to choose. I could stay with Hernan and the Spaniards or return to my home. I could genuinely embrace this Christian God or return to the many gods of my forebears. In regard to the former I quickly concluded that there was nothing for me in the place of my birth. My mother had sold me into slavery as a mere girl, and who knew what fate might await me if I returned a grown woman. I knew from the way that men of every creed and colour looked longingly at my body that I was an object of masculine desire. Surely my uncaring birth mother and her new husband would merely see me as an encumbrance or more likely a threat. So, in the end, that decision was simple, I stayed.

The question of which god or gods to follow was not so easily resolved. The difference between the beliefs these men held and how they acted was at times extreme. Maybe that was the same for all men. Though I could not read their books yet, I had spent many hours with Fray Bartholomew and the other priests being instructed in the ways of Christianity. Fray Bartholomew had tried to explain that it was indeed the same God in both the old and new 'testaments'. To my mind it seemed strange that in the old book the God was vengeful and quick to wipe out thousands, while in the new, Jesus his son was turning the other cheek.

The Spaniards constantly railed against the idols of the Maya yet they treated their blessed virgin Mary and a thousand and one saints in an almost identical way.

"Dona Marina, faith itself is a gift from God. It isn't the result of logic or careful calculation. Keep saying the prayers that I have taught you and the light of the lord will surely shine upon you." Fray Bartholomew entreated me.

I was intrigued by Aguilar's story. He himself was a priest and had somehow managed to keep his faith through long years of imprisonment and slavery, sustained by his precious tattered prayer book.

"What would have happened to you if you had lost or your captors had taken your prayer book?" I asked him.

"I know it would have made things harder, the prayers in the book were a comfort to me and a link with my homeland. But I believe that I still would have been able to sustain my faith despite its loss." He replied.

It was a dream that finally filled my soul with faith...

I was chained inside the hold of one of the great ships. There was a tremendous storm blowing and the ship was being tossed like a leaf in a tempest. I clung to the anchor point of my chains, where the chains were bolted into the thick timbers of the ship. The ship pitched violently both from side to side and backwards and forwards. Had I not been gripping the chain at its tether I would surely have been flung from side to side as if I were a discarded doll. Above, I could, in fragments catch the cries of the sailors as they cried out in despair, their cries barely audible above the rage of the wind and waves. And then there was an ear-splitting crash that sounded as if a great tree had been shattered and was falling to earth. Water began to pour into my prison, swirling like a raging river and rising swiftly up my body as I cowered against the rib of the ship. Words came to my lips unbidden:

"Oh lord Jesus save me! I will dedicate my life to your works. Please, please!"

There was a sudden stillness and the ship righted itself and became steady under my feet. The sea water that embraced my shoulders began to drain and I felt a great peace and warmth envelop me.

I awoke on my sleeping mat wet with sweat as if I was indeed half drowned. From that morning onwards I was filled with a strong faith that supported my every deed. You may think it strange that a mere dream, a mere figment of my sleeping soul, could so change me. I can only say that there have been moments in my life when I just knew what I was to do next. I didn't need to argue within my mind what the advantages or disadvantages were, the costs and benefits. I just knew.

When I had risen I went straight out to seek one of the priests. It was Bartholomew that I came to. I fell to my knees before him and cried out:

"Father, I have had a great revelation and ask for your blessing. How may I be confirmed in the path of Christ?"

It seemed to me that he was much taken aback by my sudden imploring. He composed himself saying:

"This can be done at a special mass my child. Through the power of the Holy Spirit you will receive the gifts of wisdom, understanding, knowledge, counsel, fortitude, piety, and fear of the Lord"

From that day over the next weeks I spent many hours in study of the catechism. My understanding of both the ways of the Lord and of the Spanish language was thereby greatly enhanced. Finally, I was honoured to be anointed with holy oil and at last felt as if I was as one with both Christ and my Spanish companions.

There were times as I passed through the growing town of Villa Rica de la Vera Cruz that it seemed to me that I was invisible to the men. There were other times that I felt despoiled by their eyes. At night I would sometimes stand in the shadows as groups of soldiers passed. Often enough they were in their cups, singing songs, laughing, and joking as men do when the wine has eased their throats. It was in this hidden way that I gathered the mood of the troops. Like as not they wouldn't see me, or if they did they would not realise the strength of my Spanish. As groups of the soldiers passed, I increasingly overheard complaints and grumbling.

"This expedition is a waste of time and we will have little to show for it" was a common comment. Another: *"Why has Cortes sent what little treasure we have gained back to Spain? What is the point of being in this god-forsaken place if there are no riches for us?"*

Over time these grumblings became more and more prevalent. I determined that I should let Hernan know that there was a risk of revolt among his soldiers.

I relayed all that I heard to Hernan. He confided in me that there was a small group of his men who were more loyal to the governor of Cuba, his sworn enemy Diego Velazquez, than they were to him. He thanked me for conveying this information which he had already half-guessed at. The next day what Hernan did amazed me.

"Captains!" he called out, assembling his most trusted fighters. Soon a half dozen or so of the Spanish soldiers stood waiting expectantly.

"There is a great empire for us to conquer, waiting. Are we not conquistadores? There are riches waiting that are beyond imagination. There are thousands whose souls can never be saved unless we convert them to the one true God. It is our duty to save these heretics from damnation."

Most of the men were nodding their assent as he continued:

"I shall compose letters to our king to ensure that he gives us and us alone the royal writ to conquer and govern these lands. As a sign of our loyalty and good faith we will give him not just the king's fifth but all the remaining treasures we have accumulated. Look on this as an investment in the good will of our liege that will be repaid tenfold or more. It will ensure his goodwill and our undeniable right to the untold treasures that lie in wait. We can never turn back. Our way is forward to victory or death. Therefore I order you to sink all our ships except the Maria. Strip them of all their sails, ropes and spars and set the sea into them."

There was a stunned silence. I could see the shock on the faces of the men. I wondered would they turn on Hernan and refuse to obey? If so what would become of me? I could see some of the men glancing at each other. No-one moved.

The moment passed. The most loyal of his men led by a man called Sandoval turned and headed to the small boats to carry out his orders. Gradually the rest, one by one, followed them.

The mighty and small ships were all denuded of the valuable timbers, ropes, sails and metal fittings, these were piled on the beach. Aguilar then explained to me that once all the removable items of use had been collected the hulls of the ships would be breached, allowing the sea to take them. After several hours I could see the men rowing away from the ships as one by one these mighty craft settled into the waters of the bay.

That night I didn't go to my allocated sleeping quarters.

I slipped into Hernan's quarters and as he was already on a raised platform, I stepped out of my robe and joined him. At first surprised, he then showed his pleasure with a smile and the stiffening of his organ. I ran my cupped hand gently up and down his manhood until his excitement could no longer be contained. When he entered me, I sighed, for the first time in a long time I felt as if I was at home.

In the early morning light Cortes rolled over to embrace me, tracing his fingers lightly around my face and neck before abruptly becoming all business.

"Marina, my love, I think the time has come to venture inland to meet with this Montezuma whether he wants us to or not." He declared.

"You are right Hernan; with your new allies the strength of your army is as strong as it will be for now. Your men have already come close to mutiny once and more inactivity will only feed discontent."

"Tell me about the journey to Montezuma's capital" he asked.

"The journey is very long. When I was a child I went with my father but he and I were carried on a palanquin the whole way so I didn't really experience the difficulties. Even so, I can tell you the road is long and winding, climbing high into the sky over difficult passes. The warriors who acted as porters of our palanquin had to change places many times so they could rest and not be exhausted. The air changes up there. It seems as if each breath is reduced and not enough to sustain life. It gets colder and colder, especially at night. I cannot tell you about Montezuma's military dispositions, as a child I took no notice of these things."

This reply obviously pleased Cortes as he gently kissed my forehead before rising to prepare to address his men.

When he had them assembled, he began:

"Soldiers of Spain! Warriors of Christ! Today we must prepare for our journey into the interior of this land. All we have heard has told us that wealth beyond our wildest dreams awaits us. We will bring these heathens to Christ and save their souls from eternal damnation. Tomorrow we will leave and with our shield of faith and our sword of hope we will be victorious!"

This brought about a great cheer from his men who obviously were ready for the next step. He went on to give detailed instructions to various of the captains. A garrison was to be left behind under Juan de Escalante, one of his most trusted captains. As well as around fifty fit soldiers, any of the men who were sick or wounded were to remain behind to recover. Many of the horses had also been wounded so in the end his cavalry force only numbered 15. Trusting to my description of the mountain passes they would traverse, he instructed that only the lightest of their cannons would be carried by porters. The heavier cannons and mortars were to be set in place to stiffen the defences of Vera Cruz.

That morning Hernan gave me a gift Father. Look, there they still lie in the corner of my bedroom. I lifted my weakened arm to indicate the helmet, breast plate and sword that rested against the corner of the room.

"These are for your protection my love; you are too precious for me to risk a stone striking your head or an arrow finding its way to your heart." He said. Then he told me the story of a woman called Jeanne D'Arc- a warrior woman who had once led her people to victory over an enemy people.

"You are my Jeanne D'Arc Malinali, and together we will vanquish the Aztecs." I know pride is a great sin Father but again my heart was filled with this emotion.

Chapter seven: Journey to the interior

I was impressed by the assembled force that set off the next day. Cortes and I rode at the head of fifteen cavalry, followed by several hundred Spanish troops that included the crossbowmen and harquebusiers. There were many native warriors supplied by our allies, and several hundred porters, including the remnants of the Cubans the Spanish had brought with them from that distant island.

"We will pass close to my birthplace Hernan; I have a special request" I said not long after they had left Vera Cruz behind.

"Name it" he replied.

"My nurse and my best friend Eleuia is still slave to my mother and step-father. Of all the people in this world aside from you, I love her the most. She cared for me and taught me much. I'd like to be able to free her and if she wishes have her accompany us on this journey."

There was no hesitation.

"Yes, of course my love, how far off our path is your home city?"

"Xaltipan is only a half day's walk away." I replied.

"Then I will lend you Gonzalo de Sandoval and a dozen of my strongest soldiers along with a score or more of our native allies. Gonzalo is a good man that I trust with my life. He comes from my home in Medellin, he may be the youngest of my captains but he has already shown good judgement. You may trust him as you trust me. I will give you some treasures that you might buy your friend's freedom, otherwise I will leave it to you and Gonzalo to decide whether or not to force the issue"

Sandoval and I rode while our accompanying contingent of soldiers and native warriors jogged steadily behind. Many of the soldiers, bowing to the exigencies of the climate, had by now adopted the cotton armour of the local warriors while carrying their steel breastplates and helmets at all times.

As we rode I asked Sandoval about Cortes' early life.

"We both come from a part of Spain called Medellin. That part of Spain was the last place to finish expelling the Moors, a cruel heretic people, who had occupied parts of Spain for 700 years." He began. I was curious by nature but I was more interested in learning more about Hernan.

"Tell me about Senor Cortes', his family and life, he has told me very little" I asked.

"His family were not rich, though of noble blood. He was always an adventurous lad. His father sent him off to university in Salamanca, but study was not to his taste. He came home after only a couple of years."

"And has he had many lovers?" I asked him.

At this Gonzalo laughed, replying: *"I think the senoritas have always found him attractive!"*

As I had estimated, it took only a few hours to reach my home city. My heart was in a turmoil of anxiety, what sort of reception would we get from my mother, her new lord and indeed Eli? Word had spread before us that a contingent of the strange warriors was on its way, so there was a group of warriors and an ambassador of my step-father's was waiting to greet us. I began the dialogue, wishing to assert my new position right from the start.

"Greetings, I am Dona Marina, I was born the daughter of your queen Cimatl. We come with peaceful intentions. We seek only to buy the freedom of one of the queen's slave women- Eleuia."

The ambassador was shown the gifts that included a Spanish helmet and sword and immediately sent two runners with a message for the king. It wasn't long before they returned, bringing Eleuia with them. The exchange was duly made. I wasn't at all surprised that my mother hadn't come to see me.

Eleuia came forward hesitantly. She was an old woman by now, stooped and with failing eyesight, she was puzzled why anyone would want to buy her freedom at this late stage of her life.

"Eleuia it's me Mali!" I exclaimed.

"Mali? Is it really you?" The old woman's voice was cracked like a dried leaf crushed in my hand, and hesitant.

At this I raced forward to embrace the woman who had nurtured me more than anyone in my life. At first stiff, Eleuia finally melted into my arms. As we walked towards where the two horses were tethered I said to Eli:

"There is so much that has happened since I was taken by the traders and I will tell you all, but first I want you to trust me and get up on this horse with me." I pointed to the docile mare Isabella who was waiting patiently next to Sandoval's much larger mount called Diego. Eli looked at the creatures and I could tell that she was afraid. I mounted Isabella and guided the mare in a gentle circle around Eli. Then I dismounted and led Isabella over to where Eli stood.

"See, it is perfectly safe, Gonzalo will help you get up, and you can sit behind me and hold my waist. I have ridden many miles

on Isabella and she is the gentlest, most tractable of horses. Here, come with me and look into her eyes, you will see that she is a gentle and true creature."

Taking Eli by the hand I led her to Isabella. We stood there very still while I held Isabella's head by the reins while I whispered the soft cooing sounds I'd learnt from the stable boys. Despite her fears Eli permitted herself to look into the creature's huge liquid brown eyes. Gonzalo came over with a handful of feed and I showed Eli how to hold it in the flat palm of her hand so Isabella could safely eat. Holding Eli's still trembling hand in mine I guided her to allow Isabella to eat from her hand.

"See, you are friends now" I declared.

I continued my gentle coaxing until at last the old woman relented and allowed herself to be helped onto Isabella's back behind me. At that moment I was so proud of my old friend. It is no small thing to climb onto the back of a monster after just a few minutes! She held on very hard, at first almost squeezing the air from my lungs. She was trembling with a mix of fear and anticipation. Everyone had heard about the strangers from across the sea and the huge beasts that they rode on. Never in all her years had Eli imagined that she herself would be atop one.

As we rode slowly, at the pace of the foot-soldiers, back to re-join the main column, I asked Eli about her life in the intervening years since my departure.

"I was so upset to see you go Mali!" The older woman said. "But at the same time I know your strength and cleverness; I knew that you could survive regardless of what the gods put in your way. After you were gone your mother had no further use for me. I was no longer the guardian of a princess and was relegated to nothing but the lowliest of tasks, carrying water and sweeping. No longer was I even allowed to weave or prepare food for the lord's table."

I squeezed her hand, feeling a great sorrow for the old woman.

"You are free now to do as you choose Eli" I said.

There was a long pause before Eli replied with a sad but resigned tone in her voice:

"You may say I am free Mali but what am I to do? I am an old woman now and without a master to serve I am less than worthless."

"Oh my dearest friend, you may stay with Hernan and I for as long as you live. You will want for nothing and no-one will ever tell you what to do for all the rest of your days."

Changing the subject Eli asked: "Tell me about these strangers and their ways my dear child. Are they truly gods?"

"No Eli they are certainly not Gods. They are men much like all men. They like to play and they like to fight. Some will force themselves on women, others will not. They worship a different God and are guided by their priests just as we have been guided by ours. They have an insatiable hunger for gold, they treasure it above all else, even Quetzal feathers! They are great warriors and their weapons are fearsome. They have devices called cannons that roar like thunder and cast death at a great distance. They have terrible dogs that they keep chained ready to release to rip the throats of their enemies."

"They sound truly terrifying!" Eli exclaimed.

"When their blood rage arises they are as terrible as any warrior. But they can be gentle and kind. They wish to convert all our peoples to their god. I myself have been baptised and confirmed in my faith. I have put aside our old Gods and now really wish to devote myself to the ways of Christ."

I could almost feel the turmoil that my words had created within my old mentor but went on:

"But as I have said, Eli you are now free to choose. If at some time you wish it, you will be welcomed into the company of Christ but if not you will always be under my protection."

"And what of this Hernan of whom you speak?" Eli asked.

"He is many things my dear friend. First and foremost he is a very brave and fierce warrior. He commands his men with decisiveness yet he inspires loyalty. There are some among his soldiers who I do not believe hold him dear to their hearts, but even they bow to his wishes."

"And has he forced himself on you?" Eli asked, getting straight to the point.

I was pleased that Eli couldn't see me blush.

"No, my friend, he made it clear right from the start that it was my choice to be with him or not." I paused, then continued: "I have chosen to be his woman."

From there, they rode in silence. Eli no doubt digesting all that I had told her, while I took great comfort from my old friend's bony embrace from behind.

At the end of that day's travel we re-joined the main column which had continued to make its ponderous way along the road to the city of dreams.

As I knew he would, Hernan made Eli welcome into his camp, letting her know that she was free to come and go and do as she pleased.

When they camped for the night and we were alone together, Hernan asked me: *"So how is your friend? She seems older than I'd expected."*

"I think she is fine, after I was sold into slavery she was not treated well and only given the lowliest of tasks."

"It must be a lot for anyone let alone an old woman to take in" he remarked.

"She will adjust as I have. While we say she is free to do as she pleases, what in reality is an old woman with no family to do?" I commented.

"Perhaps she will find solace in Christ, and even if not, she will at least be safe and well-fed while she is with us and I will ensure that no task is demanded of her that she does not undertake willingly" he replied.

The following day the column continued on its way towards the city of dreams.

I realised as we travelled that there were many things that I hadn't noticed on my journey with my father. On my journey with Acalan it had been he who had been pointing things out to me and explaining the various cities, forests, and wild creatures that they had passed. Now, it was I who was explaining the sights to Cortes, Gonzalo, and the other captains and priests who were in the vanguard of the column. Late in that day, near the setting of the sun, they heard a distant growling of some fierce beast.

"What is that?" asked Gonzalo.

"A Jaguar" I replied. *"Our people have always believed that the sun itself transforms into a jaguar as it slips below the horizon into the underworld. There are many jaguar gods and jaguar demigods in the beliefs of the people. We will not see him; our column is making too much noise and disturbance for him to show his face."*

When they re-commenced their journey the next day I was able to point out the changes in the vegetation as their path slowly climbed towards higher mountains. Totonac scouts were constantly running ahead of their group to provide information about what lay ahead and warn of any gathering of Aztec warriors. These Totonac warriors were fit young men who had been trained to run many miles each day without difficulty, even in the thin air they would encounter in the higher mountains that they would all soon need to climb. In the distance we could see the snow-capped dome of Orizaba, the Star Mountain, which could be seen from far and wide. Fray Bartholomew, who had studied such things, declared that this mountain must be nearly twice the height of Mount Teide, claimed to be the highest in Spain.

Our path took us ever upwards. We passed through or near many villages and towns but were unmolested. At times the road was lined with curious people who had come to witness our passage and marvel at the cavalry that they had heard so much of. Now that the air was cooler and thinner we journeyed all day long. A siesta in the middle of the day being no longer required to escape the heat of the noon sun. We attained the summit of a pass through the mountains and Hernan called a halt to address the troops and porters.

"Brothers in Christ! Together we have toiled to reach this summit, together there are many miles yet to travel. Today and in future days we will climb many heights and overcome

many obstacles. It will be hard and I have no doubt that some of us will fall by the way. But our rewards will be immense not only in this world but in the next. For we truly do Christ's work together. I name this place Puerto del Nombre de Dios and now ask Fray Bartholomew to bless our company and this place with prayers."

At this Bartholomew came forward and offered the usual incantations to bless the company and the place. All, including Eli and I, knelt and bowed our heads as the priest blessed the company and their achievements so far, seeking God's blessing on their further adventures. Eli of course understood none of this, but just followed my lead. A lifetime of servitude had inculcated in her an innate impulse to follow the lead of others. Later when we had made our camp for the night I tried to explain some of the ways of these strangers. I could tell that it was a lot for her to take in. She who had never even ventured outside our home city. But I could see the trust in her eyes and knew that she would abide by my advice. How strange it is I thought that I who had learnt so much from her, was now the teacher.

That night it rained. A cold rain that felt unlike the torrential warm rains of my birthplace. Eli and I huddled near to one of the campfires that Hernan had ordered be lit. This was colder than I can ever remember being. My body trembled and my teeth even began to bounce together. The fire provided some comfort and was kept stoked all through the night by one of the men. In the morning we discovered that three of the Cuban porters had passed into the shadows during the night. The cold of the night had come and squeezed their hearts to extinguish their lives. Poor souls to die so far from their homelands and in such a cruel and unusual manner.

The pass was not the highest point of our travails. Ahead lay another range of even higher mountains. I didn't remember it as being so steep and difficult from my childhood journey. Perhaps we'd followed a different route. Finally after a week since we'd left our coastal base we came to a wide plateau hung high in the mountains. There we found the town of Xocotlan and to the delight of all were well received by Olntetl the local chief.

"God has smiled on us Marina" Hernan declared. *"My men are exhausted by the recent weather and the endless climbing they have undertaken. We need to enjoy this chief's hospitality for a few days to regather our strength and fortitude. You were right about the change in air. Our lungs won't seem to fill, and every undertaking seems to require twice the effort."*

"Fear not Hernan, our bodies will in time learn the ways of this thin air and you will feel stronger once again" I replied in encouragement.

Olntetl the local chief was the fattest man I had ever seen or as it turned out, I would ever see. If sat alongside Tlacochcalcatl the Cempoalan leader he would have dwarfed the other man. It appeared he had no chin at all and half his head was lost in the deep folds that sat upon his shoulders. It seemed he was barely able to walk and once the mighty warriors who carried his litter had set it down he needed to be assisted if he was to move anywhere. I wondered if this excess was the result of some disorder in his body for when we later feasted he seem to eat no more than an ordinary man.

After feasting Hernan was keen, through me, to question Olntetl to discover as much as he could about the journey ahead; and as usual he was interested in the political situation of surrounding cities.

"Are you a vassal of Montezuma?" he implored me to ask.

"Who is there who is not a vassal of Montezuma" was the quizzical reply.

"You have been a most generous host to me and my men" Hernan continued, *"what peoples and cities lie ahead for me and my men, and how will we be received?"*

"You will soon enough enter into the lands of the Otomi; they are closely allied with the Tlaxcala and like the Tlaxcala maintain their independence from the Aztec though at some cost."

"What cost is that?" Hernan asked.

"Montezuma and his allies forbid trade with the Tlaxcala and any who ally with them. Tlaxcala was once very rich but year on year they diminish as the Aztec strangle them slowly"

"So they will be willing allies for our cause?"

"This is something that I would not be sure of, the Tlaxcala are fierce in their independence. You will do well to keep the peace at all costs" was Olntetl's final advice on that subject.

Turning to one of his favourite topics Hernan bade me ask: *"Is Montezuma's empire rich in gold?"* At this Olntetl gave an indulgent smile as if he were talking with a child. *"The Aztec have gold and all manner of riches that they have plundered from over 30 cities. Their wealth is beyond counting and their armies likewise. If they wish they can summon 100 000 warriors from each of their vassal cities."*

Later Hernan confided in me, and I was in agreement with him, that this was no doubt a greatly exaggerated figure. None the less it gave some sense of the power and strength of the Aztec sovereignty. For four days we rested and enjoyed the hospitality of this gigantic but generous host. On the fifth day we set out to continue our long journey to the fabled city.

Our column made its way along the length of a wide valley, moving ever closer to the borders of the Tlaxcala state itself. At the head of the valley we came to an immense stone wall at least ten feet high and more than that deep. This wall was constructed from gigantic stone blocks laid carefully atop one another and stretched from valley wall to valley wall blocking the passage of anyone seeking entry to their territory. Along the wall were emplacements designed for javelin and stone throwers alike to rain down death on those below.

Yet all was silent.

This mighty barrier, no doubt constructed to ward of Aztec intrusion, seemed unmanned.

"What do you think Marina? Should we proceed or await emissaries?"

My heart swelled a little that I was now considered in nearly all decisions that Hernan needed to make.

"Their intentions are hidden as the sun may be behind a dark cloud" I replied. *"We cannot know what this means. If we wait, we perhaps show weakness, if we proceed we may risk antagonising them. However surely if they had intended for us to wait here there would at the very least be messengers to inform us of their wishes. I think we proceed, with caution, but we must seek peace at every opportunity."*

Hernan nodded and ordered the column forward.

Within the hour we saw ahead Otomi scouts who were keeping a watch on our progress. Hernan sent a small cavalry detachment forward to capture at least one for interrogation.

As the cavalry galloped up to the Otomi they at first turned to flee. This was the expected reaction of native warriors when confronted by these huge beasts, that were likely in the warrior's eyes one creature not two. But to the great surprise of all, the warriors turned and stood their ground swinging two handed obsidian swords that slashed at the horses' throats. Two of the cavalrymen were dismounted in this way and their horses slain by blows from studded clubs and decapitated. Seeing how badly this fight was going, Hernan promptly dispatched a group of infantry and crossbow men to come to their aid. These reinforcements soon overcame the twenty or so Otomi fighters but this short savage battle had cost Hernan two horses, and a half dozen severely wounded men, one of whom, a hard to replace cavalryman, died of his wounds later.

Just as this skirmish was over we saw a terrifying spectacle. Rising up over the nearby ridge was a horde, numbering in their thousands, of Tlaxcalan warriors. Their faces were brightly painted some in red and yellow; others with long black stripes painted down their faces; and the most terrifying of all in their appearance were the many with shaven heads painted half blue half red. The battle that ensued followed the pattern of many before and many to come. The warriors charged at the Spaniards. The Spanish held their ground and slaughtered wave after wave with their crossbow bolts, harquebusier shot and most effectively by the roaring cannon. When they were at their most uncertain watching their comrades being felled in mysterious ways Hernan would send in his cavalry. The effect of these charging beasts, their armour shining bright silver, was devastating. Any of the Tlaxcalan who had not already broken and run did so with shrieks of terror.

That night we rested in the cold air of a nearby stream. Hernan was wary of further attacks and set his cannon bristling on the perimeter and ordered his cavalrymen to keep their horses saddled. The night passed peacefully enough, though I doubt anyone slept as they might have wished. In the morning Hernan consulted with his captains and determined to push on towards the Tlaxcalan capital.

That morning produced yet another skirmish with a group of Otomi warriors. We rounded a low solitary hill and I gasped at what we saw before us. The entire wide plain before us was filled with the Tlaxcalan army. Later some of the priests put their number at 40 000, I cannot know this to be a fact, to me their number was beyond count.

Eli clung to me, clearly as we all were, fearing for her life. We had both considered that we would face a particularly harsh fate should we be captured. In fact we had agreed that a quick death would be preferable.

"Father, grant me absolution for I have sinned and today I go to meet my lord!" Cried many of the men turning to the priests amongst them.

Hernan and his captains put the men into a tight quadrangle. Eli and I, mounted on the faithful Isabella were in the exact centre. I could feel Eli trembling as she clung to my waist. For one brief moment I wondered if Isabella could carry us away if the worst happened and the lines broke.

They did not. Time and time again Hernan and his captains had to rally the men and expend their tiny reserve to shore up the lines. I shall not bore you with the details of this most horrendous of battles, the most bloody any of those present had ever witnessed. Suffice to say Hernan and his men carried the day and the Tlaxcalan forces in the end retired in disarray.

That night Hernan asked me to help with the interrogation of some of the prisoners that had been taken. All but one of these captives was bowed and broken. This one was bold and boastful needing no encouragement to talk.

"I am Patli, and Xicotenga the elder is my relative, he is the great chief of all Tlaxcalan. Even as I speak to you his son Xicotenga the younger is assembling an even greater army to sweep you into oblivion. Surrender now or you will all be killed or captured to be fattened and sacrificed to the gods."

When I relayed this to Hernan he took it in his stride.

"What is your advice?" He asked.

"We must continue to seek peace" I counselled. *"The Mexica are many times stronger than the Tlaxcalan but had not managed to subdue them, if we could only win the Tlaxcala over to our side they will be powerful allies for what is to come. I think you should release the prisoners, especially this arrogant one Patli, with gifts and continued wishes for peace."*

"You do not think we will appear weak after such a great victory suing for peace?" He asked.

"Our strength is our strength Hernan. Sometimes it may be to our advantage for our opponents to believe us weaker than we are." I replied.

Once again he seemed pleased by this advice, he nodded and turned to instruct his men.

The following day there was no further attack by the Tlaxcalan forces. Instead a large group bearing gifts of food approached our encampment. Seeing that these men were unarmed, Hernan permitted them entry. They came bearing hundreds of turkeys and many many baskets of fresh maize bread. Though this visitation was a surprise, Hernan and his captains saw it for what it was: simply an effort to spy on the encampment and judge the condition of the men and horses. Acting on this belief he made sure that the gift bearers saw none of the wounded men or horses. Once again I was instructed to make offers of peace and declare that we only sought passage through their lands on our way to meet Montezuma. Hernan was at great pains to make them understand that we were not allies of the Aztec and indeed sought an alliance with the Tlaxcala against the Aztecs.

The following day we were attacked yet again, this time by what seemed an even larger force, led by Xicotenga the younger himself as we discovered later. This battle was a repeat of the previous one. It seemed to me that the Tlaxcala had learnt nothing from their previous defeat. They hurled vast numbers of warriors at the soldiers. They were so tightly packed together that the crossbow men, harquebusiers and cannoneers had no need to aim their weapons. The noise of war cries, the screaming of the wounded and unwounded, and the fearful roar of canon and muskets made such a din that the sky itself might crack. By the day's end the bodies of the slain lay in mounds sometimes four or five high.

This shattering defeat was enough, finally, to break the Tlaxcalan resolve. The following day emissaries arrived declaring that Xicotenga the younger himself wished to parlay with us.

When he made his appearance in our camp he came bearing many gifts though apologising for the quality of them.

"The Aztec have hindered our trade with other cities and so we are poorer than we once were" He declared.

"My warriors have faced the Aztec many times, and more often than not won the day. But you have proved superior in your feats of arms. We bow before you and beg your

forgiveness, it was our real belief that you were in alliance with the Aztec."

Hernan, his captains and I had already discussed how we should respond if this day ever came. All were agreed that a magnanimous response would be the most likely to gain us the alliance we so dearly needed.

And so it was agreed. The Tlaxcala after so much letting of blood became our allies. Xicotenga the younger informed us that his father Xicotenga the elder had extended an invitation for Hernan and his men to enter the city of Tlaxcala to rest, and to allow time for the wounded to recuperate.

So it was that on September 23 in the year of our Lord 1519 that we entered the city of Tlaxcala. Much preparation had gone into the city for our arrival. The road we journeyed down was lined with flowers of every colour. Priests stood in great numbers, in their hands they held pottery bowls filled with burning incense, their long dark hair matted with dried blood and fresh blood ran down their cheeks from where they had ritually cut their own ears. Great throngs of not just the city dwellers but people from all the surrounding villages came to see us. Eli and I held our heads high. We were privileged to be in the very centre of this conquering army. We and all the men were led to well-appointed quarters and for the next three weeks it seemed we were to be treated as though we were royalty. Apologetic as ever for their lack of gold and jewels, Xicotenga the Elder presented Hernan with three hundred slave girls. He took none of these for himself but distributed them amongst his men.

Over our three week stay I went everywhere with Hernan, making possible his relentless questioning of his hosts in regard to what might be expected in Tenochtitlan. Xicotenga the elder and his noblemen were clearly in awe of

Tenochtitlan. It was described as being the greatest city in the world and being impregnable as a fortress. They talked extensively of their decades long struggle to maintain their independence from the Aztec. While clearly proud of their military achievements, they made it clear that this had come at considerable cost in lives and the impoverishment of their city.

Hernan was detailed and insistent when it came to understanding as much as he could of how the Aztec fought, their tactics and weaponry, and the quality of their leadership. From this he came to understand that Montezuma himself was a priest and not a general. But the quality of his chosen generals was not in dispute. Their descriptions given in words and also in hand drawn pictures on stretched maguey fibre portrayed a very ordered and defensible city. One piece of information was taken down for particular note by Hernan's scribes: the city had only one fresh water supply from an aqueduct that began at a place called Chapultepec.

In their journeys through Tlaxcala Hernan and his captains came across many signs of human sacrifice and cannibalism. In one part of the city they found cages filled with prisoners who were being fattened. Through me he would decry such practices and declare fervently that they would burn in hell for their practices. His instinct was to draw sword and force the conversion of the city's nobility. This may not have gone well. Fortunately Father Olmedo and other wiser heads among his priests counselled a more patient approach to conversion. They even cited my own confirmation as an example of how in time a native might come of their own accord to Christ. I was happy to be used as an example. I do not know how things would have gone had he begun forced conversions.

Aztec ambassadors had arrived during our second week in the city. They came, at last, with the promise that the great lord Montezuma was willing to receive the Spanish as his guests. The route to be taken to the city of dreams was hotly debated, with Hernan in the end choosing the road that would lead through the city of Cholula.

So it was that on the tenth of October our army, much bolstered by Tlaxcalan warriors set out once more on the road. So great in number was our force that it stretched out for many miles.

Chapter eight: Massacre

Father, in my telling of this story I have, of course, been flattering in my descriptions of Hernan's, and indeed my own, actions. This is in the nature of things and bear me no ill will if I have told it from my own strongly biased view. I have turned the events that follow over in my mind many times. All I can say is that war is brutal and it changes conqueror and vanquished alike.

Our vast column was in high spirits as we set out on the road to Cholula. We were well rested, provisioned with great stocks of food, and our numbers swollen by the Tlaxcalan warriors. I had explained to Hernan and the captains that we were on our way to the most sacred city in all the world. This was the city of Quetzalcoatl himself and was visited by pilgrims from all over the known world. Eli was beside herself with excitement, she whose world had been limited to our home palace compound was going to the most sacred of cities. She chattered like a child in my ear as we rode, it was as if she was now my child and I the worldly-wise grown woman.

As we neared the city we could hear the strident sound of flutes and the blowing of conch shells. Soon enough a delegation of priests and noblemen came within our view.

"We bid you welcome to the great and holy city of Cholula" they declared. Indeed there were gifts of food, feathers, fine cloths and jewellery. The leader among them, a tall imposing man with the beak of an eagle, made it clear that all except the Tlaxcalan warriors, who had been their enemies for many years, were welcome. Hernan needed to smooth things over with the Tlaxcala by saying it was because of their fearsomeness as warriors and that the Cholulans were afraid of them. The Tlaxcalans agreed to camp outside the city and await our departure. Proof indeed of the power of flattery!

So we entered the city, Spaniards, Totonacs, the remaining Cuban porters, Eli and me.

All eyes were turned to the massive pyramid that stood astride a hill above the city. 120 steps led to the top; in the morning sunlight it shone like some divine apparition. The Cholulan welcome was initially as warm and generous as any we had encountered. We were well fed and free to wander the city and markets, marvelling at the great range of manufactured goods and produce available there. The Cholulans were without exception polite and helpful at every turn. I admired how well robed they seemed to be, even servants and slaves were clad in finely woven cloth died in bright reds, yellow and green. It was while Eli and I were examining some wonderfully crafted necklaces in the market that by chance I struck up a conversation with a Cholulan noblewoman. She introduced herself as Itzel and welcomed us back to her home. There, her generosity was boundless. Eli and I were plied with freshly cooked deer flesh, turkey, maize cakes, eggs, and fruits of every kind. I told her a little of my story and she seemed fascinated by the rise and fall, the ebb and flow, of my life. Eli was silent during much of our conversing, she told me later that she was still unused to being treated like royalty.

Over the course of many days Itzel and I became good friends. She confided in me that her husband was a captain in the Cholulan army and was away at present. Then one day she seemed troubled.

"Itzel, my friend you seem unhappy, what ails you?" I enquired.

Her face betrayed an inner turmoil as if her soul was at war with itself.

Finally she said: *"You must come away with me immediately. My husband has told me that Montezuma has ordered that the Cholulan army lay an ambush for your people. A great force has been gathered to fall on your army in a location that will be most favourable to the attackers. You, yourself will be captured and sacrificed along with any of your army who survive. Come now or all will be lost!"*

I calmly replied: *"Thank you my friend for this warning. Yes, I will come with you, but first I must return to my quarters to gather up some of my most precious possessions including a bracelet given me by my dear deceased father."*

I had told Itzel about my father and our love for one another. She agreed that I should return to my quarters to retrieve my things but bade me hurry as time was running out.

Eli and I hastened away and I quickly sought out Hernan, telling him what I had heard of the planned betrayal.

"This makes sense, my love. There has been a feeling in the air that has not chimed well with my soul. Some of my captains

have reported a furtiveness amongst the guards and have also reported that a large part of the Cholulan army seems absent."

He called together his captains to discuss how they should respond. They had all picked up on the tension in the air and none for a moment doubted my report of the planned ambush. The debate quickly shifted to what they should do next. Some suggested a return to Tlaxcala, others that they should seize the city and fortify it, still others that they seek a different route to Tenochtitlan.

Having listened he made up his own mind.

He made it known to all the Cholulan nobility and leaders that he and his army would depart in the morning. He invited them all to join him in the large courtyard of the temple of Quetzalcoatl in order for him to thank them for their generous hospitality. As they began to assemble in the main courtyard Hernan asked the most senior nobles, generals and dignitaries to join him in his adjacent quarters.

There, through me, he harangued them.

"I can see how keen you all are for us to depart your city. I know full well the trap you have prepared for us amongst the ravines that close in on the road to Tenochtitlan. Our Lord has seen fit to lay your treachery open before us. For in truth we have done nought to deserve your ire or betrayal. My men have behaved as true nobles within your city. Not one woman has been despoiled and not even as much as one maize cake has been stolen. And our reward is for you to plan our slaughter!

At this there was a confused cacophony of protestations from the noblemen. At first a few denied their intentions but in the end all claimed that their plan was all Montezuma's and as his tributaries they had no choice in the matter.

"I care not for your further falsehoods. Let this be a lesson to all who might seek to betray us!"

At this his men barred the doors and outside one of the harquebusiers fired a single shot. At this prearranged signal, cavalry galloped to bar the single remaining exit from the courtyard. From their hiding places behind pillars crossbowmen stepped out and fired volley after volley into the assembled nobility. Outside the courtyard the carnage was no less. Musket fire poured into the throng. Many tried to run and many were trampled to death by their own compatriots. There were screams and many both within and without begged for mercy. Hernan gave none. Those that reached archways were met by the cavalry and assembled pikemen. Very few were armed and the crossbowmen and harquebusiers were quick to pick off any who drew a sword or dagger. Soon all was quiet apart from the moans of a few unfortunate souls who lay waiting to die from their wounds. The courtyard ran with blood.

At Hernan's orders the city gates had been flung open and the Tlaxcala forces that had been camped outside flooded into the city. Decades of warfare between Tlaxcala and Cholula had filled them with a profound hatred of each other. I cannot describe for you the horrors that followed. I do not believe that any woman was left untouched. The screams of the city's inhabitants must have shaken even the smoking mountains. Blood ran through the streets, at times ankle deep, and building after building was set ablaze.

A few of the priests managed to escape and made their way to the top of Quetzalcoatl's pyramid. From there in utter despair they threw themselves head first down to the flagstones below. Finally, after many hours, Hernan called a halt to this hellish spectacle. A quiet descended on the city. Buildings still smouldered and there was the sound of weeping from those inhabitants who still lived. Later Bernal Diaz estimated that 5000 souls had been dispatched in those hours of madness.

That night I could not look on Hernan's face.

Eli and I shut ourselves into a separate room.

"He must be a devil my darling Mali" Eli declared.

I knew not how to answer her at that time. My mind was in such a turmoil, thoughts were racing around each other as if driven by a storm wind. When I had relayed the Cholulan plan for ambush I had never for a moment thought that this would be the result. I had by now seen more bloodshed than any should experience in an entire life but this killing of the unarmed had set my mind into confusion. I remained numb and silent. Eli wiped a tear that rolled slowly down my cheek. I still could not find words; I whose most powerful skill was that of language could not express anything. At last we lay down to rest. Eli fell asleep next to me. We took comfort in each other's familiar presence. It was many hours before my eyelids fluttered closed and I drifted into a dark dreamless sleep.

I could not look on Hernan's face for the entire passage of a day. Finally it was he and sought me out.

"You are shocked by what has happened" he rightly declared. Then continued,

"Yes I am sorry that we sent so many heathen souls to hell without being to offer them salvation. But I have now sent a clear message that will reverberate far and wide. Montezuma himself will hear of this slaughter and will be shaken out of his apathy. He will either acquiesce to our journey to his city or he will send his armies to dispatch us. He at least now knows that

we have great force of arms and will not be swayed from our course."

I nodded but not in acceptance of what he had ordered done, but rather that I could see the cruel military logic of it. Never again was this discussed between us. Forever it lay in a locked box in an empty chamber in our relationship.

Chapter nine: To Tenochtitlan

If I but had the wings of an eagle I would have been able to fly high above our column as we set out on the road to the city of dreams. It would have seemed as if a great snake was wending its way out of the shattered city of Cholula. Its head gleaming like silver as the sunshine played on the armour of the Spanish soldiers, then the bright colours of Tlaxcalan and Totonac warriors glowing in every colour, and finally the long tail of dusky porters bringing all the food, ammunition and spare weaponry. The head of the snake would slowly poke between hills and move up mountain paths dragging its long body behind it. We climbed and we climbed. Even Isabella, that most courageous of beasts, shuddered with the effort of each breath. On the steepest sections Eli and I would walk alongside her, whispering our encouragement. As we camped that night a delegation of Totonac warriors came to Hernan. They begged to be allowed to return to their homes in the coastal lowlands, never before had they been at such altitude or so far from home. Hernan was gracious. He thanked them for their service and presented them with many fine gifts of cloth, pottery and jewels in appreciation of their loyalty and in recognition of their brothers who had died along the way. He also entrusted their leader with messages for his men at Vera Cruz wishing them well and imploring them to send more powder and ammunition along the now secure supply line to the column.

With each step it seemed the air grew colder and thinner. Men would often be seen bent over coughing and wheezing as if stricken by some terrible affliction of the lungs. At night the porters suffered the most. Those from Cuba and the lowland areas were ill clad for these conditions. At night I would see them often laying together in bundles like sticks to keep warm. Also at night the thickest blankets were layered over the horses and our men slept in every item of clothing they could find, they also covered themselves in any scrap of cloth they could find.

Yet there was wonder. We soon passed near to the two great fiery mountains, Popocatepetl, he whose name means hill that smokes, and Iztaccihautl the white woman. Hernan sent Diego de Ordaz to investigate the heights of White Woman with a small group of men. They were gone for a full day and night but on their return they had quite a story to tell. They emerged into our campsite looking like ghosts, they were covered from head to feet in grey ash, their normally black beards and hair turned grey by the journey.

"We climbed and climbed, stumbling over rocks and breathing air that grew even thinner giving us no sustenance. Snow and ice fell on us in swirling assaults, mixing with fine ash that covered us from head to foot, in the end I left all but one companion behind to rest and ventured forth." Diego reported.

"Soon enough my companion and I were jumping over rivers of lava and the air became so hot it burnt our mouths and lungs. At times the earth beneath our feet would tremble and we needed to crouch low lest we topple. In the end it grew so hot that our clothes began to catch fire and we could go no further. On our descent the clouds that had enveloped us parted briefly and we could see the way forward and a vast city spread out across a lake."

Hernan congratulated Diego and his companions for their bravery and for the useful information about the best path to take. And so we set off, following the direction that Diego had indicated would be the easiest and most straight forward. We had travelled barely a half day when we came to a fork in the road. One branch of the fork had been barricaded over with boulders and large tree trunks. Hernan had captured a couple of Aztec guides and sought their recommendation as to which way to go. Of course when they advised the unbarred road he chose the other. Our remaining Cuban porters and our Tlaxcalan slaves were set to work clearing the road, they had barely begun to do so when we were hit by the first storm of Winter. A great wind began blowing, bringing with it at first sharp stinging rain, then thick flurries of snow. Hernan ordered that the work be halted and that everyone should seek what shelter they could find. For myself I was grateful that Eli and I were permitted the use of a nearby abandoned hut. So we spent the night in relative comfort while Spaniard, Tlaxcalan and Cuban alike had to make do with the cover of crudely made shelters that they constructed from fallen branches. All night the wind howled and Eli and I held each other close in the relative comfort of our abode while all others shivered outside.

In the morning though the storm had gone on its way, the sun was shining reflecting brightly off the fresh carpet of snow that had been laid for us in the night. After a breakfast cooked on fires that we all huddled around, we set off, once again climbing steadily though not steeply. As we reached the summit of the rise we were climbing, the warmth of the sun was making ghostly forms of mist that were born and then drifted away. Reaching the top we looked down into the valley of Mexico to see the most wonderful sight. The great city of Tenochtitlan lay spread out beneath us like the most wondrous work of art. Azure waterways snaked between groups of buildings that were painted in bright white. The effect was magical as the houses and larger buildings seemed to float on the blue of the water as if held up by some hidden force. Woodsmoke drifted lazily from many houses to be enveloped in the patches of mist that wandered across the surface of the lakes. Around the edges of the lakes were miles and miles of cultivated fields, many bright green with bean crops, others tinged with gold from ripened maize. Wide irrigation channels criss-crossed these fields in unerring straight lines. I do not remember being so impressed by my first views of the city of dreams when I was a child. Perhaps we had come by another road, or perhaps having seen so many other cities now as a grown woman, I had come to a better appreciation of its brilliance. Eli was clearly also stunned by the city's beauty. She held my hand tightly and I could hear her muttering prayers to many gods as we stood.

We began our descent and with each step it seemed the surroundings became more civilised. We passed through many small villages which were neatly organised and well cared for, we were greeted by crowds of on-lookers who were neither hostile nor friendly, they merely stared. At last we reached the small town of Amecameca where Hernan decreed that we should rest and spend the night. In the morning we were met by an Aztec delegation who told us that Montezuma himself was coming to greet us. Sure enough after an hour or so we could hear the sounds of flutes and conch shells as a large party approached us.

We waited in anticipation as a palanquin was set down, cloths laid out and a finely dressed man stepped down. He was dressed in blue robes and from his back appeared to spring Quetzal feathers in abundance. Porters brought forth a vast array of gifts including a huge haul of golden objects. The captains examined these gifts and in the particular the gold, which seemed to affect them in the same way as drinking too much wine. They laughed and smiled and passed the objects to each other drooling with delight.

I was looking at this Montezuma and my brow was furrowed. When I had been to the city as a child I had only seen the

Emperor from some distance but this man looked wrong. I remember Montezuma as seeming taller, more slender, and even with the passage of years much younger than he who stood before us.

"Senor Cortes, I believe you are being tricked" I said. *"I know I was but a child when first I came here, but this man does not fit my recollection of Montezuma."*

Hernan turned to one of the Tlaxcalan warriors who had been taken prisoner and then traded back by the Aztecs. The man confirmed the deception. Later we learnt that the man who had presented himself before us was a nobleman called Tziuacpopocatin who Montezuma had instructed to impersonate him. It seems the emperor's thought was that by deceiving us into thinking we had met him and received many golden gifts we would turn back the way we had come. There was to be no turning back.

In the end we stayed in Amecameca for an extra day. The city 's chiefs were most hospitable showering Hernan with many gifts, including another forty slave girls who were duly distributed amongst the men. I was able to negotiate very good relationships with the city's leadership. As they came to trust us they became more and more open about how they suffered under the weight of the Aztec, or Mexica as they referred to them, and the taxes and tributes that were imposed on them.

After these two restful days we continued on, reaching the shores of Lake Chalco, the first of the chain of connected lakes that led to lake Texcoco and the city of dreams. The city here was vibrantly full of life and its inhabitants numbered many thousands. It was here that the Spaniards for the first time saw the extent of water borne commerce that the lakes supported. The canals of the city and the lake waters fairly buzzed with the coming and going of hundreds of canoes and small boats. Traders and farmers alike filled their craft with fresh produce, woven cloth, pottery, household implements and all manner of valuables. It was here that we were approached by a truly noble ambassador. A palanquin carried on the shoulders of men, who were themselves chiefs of towns, arrived bearing Montezuma's nephew who himself was king of the city of Texcoco.

Cacama was of great bearing. A strong, handsome, and well-muscled man with sharp intelligent eyes and accompanied by a finely attired retinue. His litter was decorated with many of the prized Quetzal feathers, on its side were designs in the form of fine trees shaped in silver and gold that bore precious jewels of many colours as their fruit.

"My lord Montezuma, who is as the sun itself, has sent me to welcome you to our kingdom. He bade me offer his deepest apologies for not being present himself but unfortunately he is unwell just now. I Cacama, nephew of the great Montezuma and king of Texcoco bid you welcome. It will be my pleasure to escort you first to the city of Iztapalapa and from there to the capital itself. There you will be well received and my uncle will surely grant you an audience."

At this Hernan and his captains' faces expressed great relief and delight that their three month journey from Vera Cruz was at last to reach its ultimate destination.

With our august guides taking the lead and our long tail stretching out behind us we set off.

Soon enough we came to the first of many causeways that we would encounter. This one was straight as an arrow's flight, constructed entirely of stone, and leading for five miles across the lake. The causeway was narrow, I could tell that Cortes felt that he and the army were very exposed being strung out only two or three abreast for miles. However the transit passed without incident and we arrived safe and sound at the city of Iztapalapa the city of Montezuma's brother Cuitlahuac, uncle of Cacama.

We were led to richly appointed villas that were to serve as our homes for a few days. With my adult eyes I saw many things that I had paid no heed as a child. The houses were all two or three levels with fine kitchens, sleeping rooms, and wonderful outdoor gardens. Every space was connected to others by wide corridors lined with fragrant herbs and flowers. Half the city hung out over the lake so that at times it gave the impression that it floated as if by some strange magic.

"This city is a marvel!" Hernan declared to his captains. *"The skill of the builders, the cleverness of the architect exceeds anything to be seen in any city in Spain."*

Yet despite the warmness of the welcome Hernan and his leaders seemed wary. They were clearly few compared to the numbers Montezuma could muster should he turn against them. Hernan instructed his men that at all times they should be battle ready. At night guards were to be posted to keep watch at all times. Despite their caution the Captains took the opportunity to explore the city accompanied by their Mexica guides.

On our third day in the city we received word that Montezuma was ready to receive us and that we were to proceed along the much wider causeway that linked Iztapalapa with Tenochtitlan itself.

Oh how our hearts beat with excitement within our breasts. At last we were to be received by the great lord Montezuma and be welcomed into the great city of dreams.

As a child, on my visit with my father, I had paid no heed to the defensive dispositions of the city, but now after witnessing so many battles I paid great heed. We came up to a vast wall flanked by tall towers and passed over a great drawbridge that could be lifted in times of war. The immense gates were open for us and so on November the eighth 1519 we entered the city.

The delegation that met us began to instruct us on how to behave in the presence of the great king. They treated me with much suspicion. I could tell by their looks and stolen fragments of their conversation that they knew not what to make of me. Was I a goddess with my knowledge of many tongues and riding alongside the Spanish leader as an equal?

As we waited I could sense the tension in Hernan. I turned to him as we dismounted.

"Are you well my love?" I asked softly.

"Yes, my wonderful one" he replied, *"But I can hardly believe that we are here at last, 9 months after leaving Cuba and three from Vera Cruz we have finally arrived."*

He was right to be overawed, here we were, a small band of soldiers at the threshold of the largest city in all the world.

Two columns of nobles approached and in their centre was a mighty litter bearing Montezuma. His litter itself must have contained more wealth than a small city. It was plated in gold on the outside. On the inside silver, gold and precious stones were encrusted onto every surface, brilliant quetzal feathers waved from every surface. When the litter had stopped noblemen swept the ground before the finest cloaks were laid out several layers thick in preparation for the touch of his feet.

Montezuma approached, flanked by Cacama and Cuitlahuac. All the nobles were barefoot but Montezuma's feet were encased in golden sandals. I stood back, leaving Hernan to stand alone to meet this most high of kings. I had never seen Montezuma up close before. He was indeed an impressive figure. He was well muscled and clearly carried great physical strength, his manner entirely regal and his eyes deep and calm. His cloak was studded with jewels and embroidered with gold, and on his head the most magnificent headdress adorned with Quetzal feathers. His lower lip held a blue stone hummingbird, his ears adorned with turquoise and his nose with deep green jade.

Hernan stepped towards him to embrace, as is the Spanish way. Cacama and Cuitlahuac were quick to gently restrain him, for none could touch Montezuma and only the most noble could look on his face.

Hernan was characteristically bold, through me he asked directly *"are you Montezuma?"*

There was a pause, I wondered if his directness had offended the great emperor but the reply was calm and simple *"Yes, I am he"*.

They walked together a short distance along the street and Montezuma motioned to one of his followers who brought forth a cloth wrapped gift. This was a necklace of red shells and finely wrought gold that he presented to Hernan. In addition all the captains and I were presented with garlands of sweetly scented flowers. Then Montezuma commanded

"You must all be tired after your long journey. I have followed your progress with great interest, and I know of the travails you have undergone. I have ordered that the palace of my deceased father, Axayacatl, be prepared for you and your men.

I go now to pray to my gods that I may receive their wisdom in all things."

He turned to go, and by this we knew that our first audience with him was now over.

Chapter ten The greatest of all cities

Cacama and his attendants led us to the currently unused palace. Here we were allocated quarters according to our rank. The Captains and Hernan all had individual villas of varying sizes that were ranged around a wide central plaza. The soldiers were all allocated smaller houses though even these were all in good condition and satisfactory for their needs. The porters and slaves were gathered up under cloth shelters, even the horses were given beds of herbs and flowers!

When all had settled into their appointed quarters Hernan ordered one of the now familiar, at least to me, military displays. The soldiers lined up in tight formations flashing their swords, the cavalry galloped in a tight circle and as the grand finish the harquebuses and falconers rent the air with their thunder. The smoke from their discharges drifted across the crowds watching causing them to cough and hold their noses.

Later that afternoon Montezuma summoned Hernan and four of his captains to meet him in his own palace, I of course was privileged to attend. Hernan was given a seat right next to Montezuma's gold encrusted throne, while the Captains and I were seated on a level a few steps down. The royal palace was a very new complex, the walls were all smooth and carefully painted with white wash, richly embroidered banners hung down from the walls, many were portraying Montezuma's own coat of arms, an eagle attacking a jaguar. It seemed to me that Montezuma wished to understand his visitors, and in particular to settle in his mind the question that had troubled him since news had first arrived of the Spanish landing. Were these strangers Gods? And in particular was Hernan Quetzalcoatl, the feathered serpent, returned to claim his rightful kingdom?

We were again presented with many gifts, the quantity and quality of which was beyond compare. Once again I witnessed how the Captains seemed to become intoxicated at the sight of much gold as if they had consumed too much pulque. Montezuma gave a long speech that to my mind rambled, I could tell by his words that he was deeply troubled by the appearance of these strangers. At the end of his speech, Hernan gave a short one proclaiming his friendship and saying how long he and his men had longed to meet the great king and set their eyes on his fabulous city.

At the conclusion of this meeting Montezuma indicated that he would provide guides so that the Spaniards could roam his city freely and look on its greatness. He declared his intention to retire to the main temple and offer prayers to Huitzilopochtli the unfailing god of war

That night, Hernan, ever cautious once again instructed that guards were to be set at all entrances to the palace. The night passed without incident.

The following morning we were once again invited to meet with the great king. As before Montezuma was seated on his throne and Hernan was near to his side but lower. Hernan instructed me to explain our religious beliefs to the Aztec lord. With some assistance from Hernan I talked about our Lord and how he gave his son to save humanity. Hernan wanted me in particular to stress how abhorrent human sacrifice was to us.

Montezuma replied

"I have heard from my ambassadors much about your religion. I know you are constantly seeking my people to follow in your ways. But I tell you here, our gods have served us well. Our people have prospered and brought stability to many different tribes across this land. Our prayers and sacrifices have ensured

the rising of the sun each morning and the bountiful crops that our fields provide for us. I do not expect that you will turn aside from your God and neither should you expect us to turn away from ours."

This was said with great dignity and peacefulness. I had been told that Montezuma was a man of profound belief and that he sought guidance from the gods for every major decision.

I knew that no words would sway Hernan, the captains and the priest from their fervent desire to convert all they came in contact with to Christianity. I know that their hearts were genuine in this urge, truly, and I came to share it, in the knowledge that without turning to Christ there could be no entry into heaven. This would certainly not be the last time that matters of religion would be discussed between us.

The next few days were spent exploring the wonders of the city of dreams. Hernan insisted that our quarters were to be guarded at all times and that despite the kindness and hospitality of our hosts no chances were to be taken.

The central marketplace was beyond our wildest dreams. Around 60 000 people were engaged in the buying, selling and trading of every conceivable item of food, clothing, pottery and jewellery. Hernan and the other Spaniards were most intrigued by the jewellery section where images of every creature on earth fashioned from gold silver and jewels were to be found. More than once I heard the men commenting that the quality of craftsmanship far exceeded anything to be found in Spain. I myself was fascinated by the menagerie that Montezuma had assembled for his amusement. Here were to be found jaguars, mountain lions lynxes, wolves, snakes, lizards and crocodiles. In cages birds of every kind, many strutting in the glory of their bright plumage, were housed for the enjoyment of the lord and his nobles.

We made many later visits to Montezuma's palace and were granted the privilege of touring his entire palace. The palace was set high above other buildings in the city so that he could survey his great city laid like a carpet before him. The scale of the palace was more than anyone had ever envisaged. Eli was permitted to accompany me on one of these tours and she, who had only seen her home city and that of Tlaxcala remarked that it would be sufficient for a hundred great lords. The palace was guarded at all times by 3000 warriors and Montezuma himself was attended by 1000 slave women, hundreds of whom were allegedly his concubines. At mealtimes hundreds of dishes were prepared for him to choose from, and when he had supped, he would sit with his pipe and a bowl of hot chocolate engaged in quiet conversation with his priests and advisers.

There was so much to see in the city and even beyond, for it was a miracle to sit and look across the mirror surface of the lake, it was as if the city were the greatest of ships anchored to the shore. The soldiers were very impressed watching a game of tlachtli in the specially constructed ball courts. This sport, played by noblemen only, required a high level of skill. The participants would seek to pass a rubber ball through stone hoops placed high on the walls of the court using only elbow and hips. The players wore leather knee, shoulder, elbow and chin guards to protect them from the assaults of their opponents, truly no quarter was given!

Not all the sights of the city were pleasing to the eye.

My friend, Gonzalo de Sandoval, who had accompanied me on my journey to rescue Eli, returned from the city with a disturbing story.

"We were shown to a place much like a theatre. But where an audience might be seated there was row on row of skulls, by

my guess over 130 000 at least. They were bleached white as if they were made of alabaster. Their heads and eyeless sockets all pointed towards an open space where some play or entertainment might be performed. As I looked on this strange and hideous sight I truly felt a chill run down my spine."

This was not the only sight that was to horrify my Spanish companions. You may think me callous Father but for me sacrifice had been a normal part of life. Until I turned to Christ I accepted that it was as necessary as eating and drinking to maintain life, the rising of the sun, and the health of crops. Hernan was morbidly curious to see more of the religious practices of the Aztec. He frequently beseeched the lord Montezuma to permit a visit to the great temple of the city wherein lay the place of Huitzilopochtli. In the end this request was granted and Montezuma declared that he personally would escort his honoured guest. The small entourage that would be permitted included Hernan, myself, Christobal de Olid, and seven of the Spanish soldiers.

At the base of the mighty pyramid we were instructed to wait. Montezuma arriving on his litter had his way swept and covered as was the custom. He then ascended the steep steps to the temple on the summit and disappeared from view. We were unsure if we were intended to follow or await further instruction. Presently a number of dark robed priests came down the steps to assist us in our climb. The steep steps were intended to ensure that a body flung from the summit would plunge unhindered into the courtyard below. Despite the time we had spent since leaving the thick air of the coast our lungs had not yet learnt to draw enough air and all were huffing and puffing when we reached the top.

Hernan made a great show of surveying the magnificent view out across the entire valley of Mexico as he settled his breath.

Knowing him as I did, I knew he would be memorising every causeway, road and bridge should he need that knowledge in a future conflict. We were led across a smooth courtyard into the two shrines that crowned the summit. The first honoured Tezcatlipoca whose stone statue portrayed him as a standing jaguar with a cloudy mirror grasped in one hand and a studded club in the other. We then entered the sanctum of Huitzilopochtli, a privilege granted to few mortals. The first thing that struck us in the almost darkness was the rancid smell. The stone image of the god stood before us, eyes bright with jewels, hands clasping golden bow and arrows. The form was covered in splatterings of blood, some fresh some long dried. In the half-light we could see other statues of snakes, dragons and demon like creatures gathering like a crowd of horrors around. The priests with their ghost-like white faces and their hair tangled with dry blood seemed to crowd closer. Even I who had seen much felt like running from that place, but we all held our nerve. Beyond the statues our eyes could now make out a series of braziers burning with a low glow, sitting on the hot coals were human hearts, some fresh, that sizzled and contributed to the almost overwhelming stench.

Through me, Hernan spoke to Montezuma

"You are a solemn and learned lord. How can you not see that that these creatures you worship are not gods but rather the opposite, they are devils freshly risen from the fires of hell."

He boldly went on to request that he be allowed to create a small chapel nearby. To all of this Montezuma did not immediately reply, merely staring directly at Hernan as if to bore through him with his eyes. At last he spoke

"I would not have brought you here had I known you would insult our ways in this manner. Have I not allowed you to

continue with your worship of your gods and provided you with every hospitality?"

He motioned with his left hand and we were led away back down to the foot of the pyramid. He did not accompany us.

Hernan had often implored that he be allowed to build a chapel and confided in me that he thought this request would now never be granted. But to our surprise an envoy came to us the next day informing us that we could proceed to build one in a designated area of our palace's courtyard. Montezuma even sent stone workers and builders to assist in its construction. The building proceeded at pace and soon enough Bartolome de Olmedo and Juan Diaz were able to hold a mass in a consecrated place right in the heart of the empire of the Mexica.

It was during the construction of the chapel that one of our own builders accidentally discovered a secret passageway in an adjoining building. This corridor showed signs of having only relatively recently being blocked off. Under the supervision of Hernan it was secretly opened up that night. Bearing torches the captains entered in some trepidation. But within what they found was not some ghoulish assembly of demonic idols, but more treasure than any had ever rested their eyes on before. Piled carelessly on each other were golden bejewelled treasures the quantity and like of which had never before been seen.

The captains would have gladly carried it all out to share with the men and take their own. But Hernan would have none of it. He ordered the passage to be resealed and forbade any to speaking of its discovery. The men were not happy but he promised them that this treasure and more would be theirs in the fullness of time.

Chapter eleven: Ruler in chains

Eli and I had been exploring the endless maze that was the city's markets accompanied, as always, by our Aztec guide and my bodyguard of three of Hernan's finest men. When he had allocated my guard he had simply said that I was far too valuable to him in far too many ways for him to take any risk with my safety. On our return to the palace I could tell immediately that there was something wrong. Hernan and his captains were all in a huddle fervently discussing something. I was now as accepted a member of the leadership as his most trusted captain. Approaching, I asked

"What has happened? I can tell that there is something wrong."

"We have received news from Vera Cruz that Juan de Escalante is dead."

"What happened?"

"An Aztec force lured him out of the fortress, they attacked him and while at the time he was wounded, he has since died of his wounds. Six other men were also killed and one of the horses. I've been told that one of the men was captured alive, sacrificed, and that Montezuma was sent his head impaled on a pole."

In his hand Hernan held a letter from Vera Cruz that set out the whole sequence of events. I could see that his rage boiled, at such times his eyes narrowed and his jaw took on a certain set. He immediately sent a messenger requesting an audience with Montezuma. So it was that before the setting of the sun that day we were once again meeting with the emperor, leader of the triple alliance.

Hernan had assembled five of his captains and thirty men armed to the teeth. In his pocket he kept the letter from Pedro de Ircio who was now commanding the Vera Cruz fortress. Montezuma was, as we had learnt to expect, gracious in his greeting and offered many gifts. But then Hernan's face became hard and he withdrew the letter from his breast pocket.

He got straight to the point.

"I have received word from my fortress at Vera Cruz that one of your men has attacked my commander and killed many of my men and one of my horses. This leader of yours, one Qualpopoca, was acting on your direct orders this letter informs me."

He was now standing as close to Montezuma as was permitted, almost waving the letter in his face. I could tell that Montezuma's nobles and guards were much affronted by his vociferous manner. But then he switched to a more conciliatory tack.

"I cannot believe that you would have ordered such a treacherous act my lord, but none the less this grave matter must be looked into more fully. I have no desire to start a war and destroy your magnificent city over this issue but I must insist that you come with me to our quarters. You will be looked after as if you were in your own palace but if you do not you will be killed here and now by my men."

We were all, Aztec and Spaniard alike dumbfounded by the sheer audacity of this move.

The silence hung in the air like cannon smoke.

At last Montezuma, with the great dignity to which I had become accustomed, replied

"I have no knowledge of this matter that you have accused me of. I will instruct that Qualpopoca be brought here for interrogation." So saying he removed a wonderful jade bracelet from his wrist. *"This can go with my messengers to ensure instant obedience to my wishes."*

Hernan replied, *"That is indeed a good plan, but I still insist that you come into our care until the matter is resolved."*

To which Montezuma replied, *"I am not one who can be imprisoned, were I to consent to it my people would rise up in anger."*

He then even offered his two daughters and his son as alternate prisoners. The discussion went on and on with each equally insistent on their standpoint. I could hear the captains getting restless with this endless back and forth. Velazquez de Leon even went as far to say *"Words, words, words, what is the use of them? Either we take him now or he can die by the knife. We must act now or we will all join the dead."*

His tone was so sharp that Montezuma asked me to translate his words for him.

This I did and then I added *"My lord, I have travelled with these men for many months and witnessed many battles. I have no doubt that they will carry out their threat and your blood will be spilt if you do not submit."*

To my surprise he then agreed to accompany Hernan and the men on the condition that every effort was to be made to ensure that to all outward appearances he had done so of his own volition. So it was that the greatest ruler on this earth became the prisoner of our small band of warriors.

About three weeks later Qualpopoca arrived back from the coast accompanied by his son and fifteen chiefs. Qualpopoca could scarcely believe it when he was handed over to Hernan's men for questioning. In the end after an interrogation that I would now call torture he admitted to his part in the killing of the Spanish troops.

The next morning seventeen stakes were erected in the courtyard right in front of the great temple. These were surrounded by piles of wood of all kinds and Qualpopoca and the others were bound to the stakes. Montezuma himself was chained in iron and taken to view the proceedings, never in my or anyone's imagination had we foreseen that the emperor god would be treated with such callous indignity. I averted my eyes as Hernan and two of his captains approached the stakes with burning torches. One by one the torches were touched to the piles and the flames began to embrace the captives. Though my head was averted I could not block out the screams of the dying men and the horrid smell of burning human flesh that seemed to cloy to every part of my skin.

So it was that Hernan sent an ominous message to any who would oppose the will of Spain.

Afterwards Montezuma was taken back to his well-appointed quarters and Hernan knelt before him and released him from his chains. To me the great leader of the Aztec seemed now a broken man. Tears streamed down his cheeks and he seemed unable to speak.

The situation that now developed was the strangest imaginable. Hernan permitted, nay even encouraged, Montezuma to continue to rule his kingdom. Envoys came and went, festivals were held, and Montezuma continued to feast fast and pray as he had always done. But at all times the sharpest of Hernan's men were nearby and ready to take action if there were to be any attempt to escape. Word also came to the palace that Cacama in particular was restless and might be plotting to overthrow his uncle and dispatch the Spaniards.

Yet for five months there was a period of relative inactivity. Montezuma and Hernan spent much time together. Can I say they became friends? I'm not sure. I knew Hernan well enough that he was always planning and looking for the next opportunity. His men made a map of the city, the location of the great causeways, the bridges and drawbridges that would control access, and the massive aqueduct that fed the city its water. These observations led Hernan to conclude that control of the waterways could mean control of the city.

To give him the edge he and his captains devised a plan. They would construct boats in the Spanish style that could carry some of the cannon and many harquebusiers and crossbow men. He put a bright young man called Martin Lopez of this project telling him that whatever he needed to complete the plan would be his. Some of the ship's tackle that had been saved from the scuttled ships in Vera Cruz harbour was sent for. It took four weeks for the masts, ropes, sails, anchors, pulleys and so on to arrive. By the time they came Martin had already supervised the construction of the hulls of the four lake ships. Each was to be fitted with a mast and sails but also heavy oars. Martin had concluded that the winds were not consistent and there were places in some of the canals where the magnificent buildings blocked the passage of the breeze. Each ship was fitted with heavy cannons, four to a ship, and could carry up to 75 men. In all the project took just over three months to complete.

Hernan invited Montezuma to enjoy a "pleasure cruise" on the lake but I have no doubt the great lord saw through this childish duplicity. None the less Montezuma went along and was duly impressed with the speed and manoeuvrability the craft. Once clear of the landing the sail was unfurled and soon began to fill with the power of the wind. Soon enough the cleverly designed ship was racing along at a pace that even the swiftest of Montezuma's canoes couldn't match. From then on the brigantines sailed back and forth exploring the entirety of the lake regions.

This was not the only trip together that Hernan and the emperor took. At times they would go into the forest, always accompanied by the Spanish guards, and hunt for deer, rabbits and wild fowl. Hernan showed Montezuma the workings of a musket and for his part Montezuma told his attendants to show the Spaniards how their blowpipes operated. All seemed very convivial, but it also felt like a time out of place, and that at any moment a tempest would come and shatter this fragile peace.

I cannot believe how compliant Montezuma had become. It was as if he had lost his will and was now totally subsumed to the iron will of his Spanish master. Word came that Cacama, who had always been a firebrand, was plotting a coup of some sort. This word came to us via Montezuma himself who seemed now to be seeking to avoid bloodshed at any cost. Perhaps he was so in Hernan's thrall that he genuinely believed that despite their overwhelming strength in numbers the Aztec could not overcome the Spanish force of arms. Having told Hernan of Cacama's plotting he assisted him in the luring of Cacama to an ambush where Cacama was captured and taken prisoner. He was replaced by his brother Coanacochtzin who was totally compliant to Montezuma's wishes.

It was after this remarkable series of events that Hernan said to me *"Marina my love. I think the time has come to seek the fealty of the Aztec to the king of Spain. I will ask Montezuma to bring together all the most important leaders of the triple alliance so that they may pledge their allegiance. I will need your wonderful grasp of languages and what lies hidden in men's hearts to help me ensure they are genuine in this."* I could barely believe that he was now expecting this mighty empire to bend its knees to a King who resided so far across the sea, and who had only sent such a paltry force. Yet so it was to be.

Four days later the nobility of Mexica were assembled and Montezuma addressed them.

"My noble and loyal lords, I have been your ruler for eighteen years. In that time our grasp has reached far and wide and our dominion lies over more land than has ever been unified in rule before. We all know of the prophesy that strangers would arrive in great floating houses from lands unknown that lie far to the East. I have spent many days in prayer and consultation with the gods to seek the truth. Indeed Huitzilopochtli would not have permitted my capture had it not been the will of the gods. I now..." and here he hesitated and I could see tears flowing freely down his noble face..." *I implore you to offer gifts and obey the wishes of King Charles V who is lord of faraway Spain and from this time onwards shall be our lord".*

To my amazement one by one the assembled lords complied. Most I believed because of their love for Montezuma, others, especially those held in chains, out of fear of the Spanish. I know that the burnings had been reported far and wide and must have carried great import on their rank smelling odour.

Chapter twelve: Adversity

From the day of the swearing of allegiance the flow of gold and treasures into the coffers of the Spanish became a torrent. At Montezuma's order collectors were sent to all parts of the empire to bring back the finest of everything. I've never cared much for gold but truly, as Hernan had once said, the Spanish had some sort of gold sickness of the heart. As the wonderfully wrought necklaces, bracelets, plates and ornaments arrived they were melted down into blocks known as ingots. It seemed a pity to me that what had taken a craftsman so long to create, perhaps the finest hummingbird, its wings aflutter, should be returned to a solid lump.

Hernan had a steady stream of messengers travelling back and forth to Vera Cruz, he also had supply trains bringing what was left of his dwindling stock of arms to Tenochtitlan. It was a swift messenger riding hard on one of the precious remaining horses that brought him the worst of all news. At first he would not tell me the cause of the thunderclouds that hovered on his brow. But when I pointed out that there was very little that had been achieved without my support he relented.

"I have received word of the arrival of a fleet of eighteen Spanish ships at the coast near Vera Cruz."

"Surely that is good news? Has the king of Spain sent you reinforcements?" I asked.

"These men are not directly from Spain. They are in the service of Diego Valazquez the governor of Cuba and they have come to seize from us all that we have gained through so much hardship and suffering." He replied.

Father, the thing you must understand is that Hernan was a man of action. There was no challenge he ever met that he shrank from. Where others might prevaricate he took action.

He called his captains together at once and gave them the news and his plan.

"Brothers we have fought not just native armies but also the cold winds of the mountains and the trials of hunger and thirst. That pig Valazquez would take it all from us. We must respond at once. We shall leave a force of 120 men under Captain Pedro de Alvarado to maintain our control of Montezuma and the capitol. The rest of us will march to the coast immediately. I will call back all our scouting expeditions and have them meet us at the city of our loyal allies the Tlaxcala. From there we will go to confront the leader of this expedition Panfilo de Narvaez."

I could see that this was a gamble, eighteen ships would have brought many more troops than Hernan had started out with, and dividing his already weakened force would mean that he would be greatly outnumbered. Leaving just 120 men behind would also undermine our position in the Aztec capitol.

He turned to me *"Dona Marina will accompany me, her knowledge of languages and her ability to gather allies to our flag will be essential."*

And so we set out without hesitation to retrace our steps. But even as we were preparing to enter the great causeway another group arrived from the coast. They consisted of two Spanish and a group of Tlaxcalan warriors and porters but what they carried was of great interest. Bound in nets of vines were three of Narvaez's men, this unfortunate trio had been captured by the loyal Sandoval and sent to the great city. Hernan had them released and spent an hour or so in earnest discussion with them. He sent Father Olmedo to gather much gold and treasure to offer to them as a bribe to make them change sides. Oh truly the souls of these men can be bought and sold for an ounce of the shiny golden metal!

Olmedo and the three were sent ahead with a considerable haul of gold with instructions to see if they could covertly win any more of Narvaez's men to our cause.

Montezuma came, borne on his litter, to bid us farewell. He had offered Hernan warriors but Hernan had refused declaring that *"I need only the help of our Lord Jesus Christ, with his shield and sword we will prevail"*. How odd it was to watch Hernan and Montezuma embrace as though they were truly brothers, not captor and captive.

Our long period of rest and recuperation in the city of dreams had left the men fit and raring to go. We made excellent time retracing our path back to Cholula where we met up with the returning scouting parties that Hernan had called back. All up we now numbered more than 300 but considerably less than 400. Hernan sent riders on to Vera Cruz to ensure that the garrison knew that we were on our way. As we marched and rode out towards Tlaxcala we met father Olmedo and the three Narvaez Judas's.

"Dear Father, tell me of what you have found in regard to Narvaez and his force" Hernan asked.

"He has a large force, more than twice as many as ours" Olmedo replied. The dismay that this might have brought was tempered when he continued *"We have distributed much gold among dissidents in his army, and there are many of them. I do not think it impossible for you to tip the scales in your favour with luck and the will of God."*

Hernan was clearly pleased with this piece of information, less so with the next as Father Olmedo continued:

"I have heard that Montezuma has been in secret communication with Narvaez. They have reached an

agreement that Narvaez will free Montezuma in return for his support in capturing or killing your good self, sir."

The look on Hernan's face turned as dark as night. I could tell that neither Narvaez nor Montezuma would receive any mercy.

We marched on to Tlaxcala. There we were met by the loyal Sandoval who had secretly marched out of Vera Cruz to bring some additional soldiers and some new weapons. He had ordered his craftsmen to make long lances with copper blades that could be used against Narvaez's cavalry if need be. I knew that Hernan would feel the loss of even one of the precious horses. I knew though by now that he would stop at nothing to attain his goal.

My dear friend Sandoval also brought word that Narvaez was ensconced in Cempoala and was on good terms with our erstwhile friend the fat chief Tlacochcalcatl. The discussion between captains was loud and vociferous that night. In the end a decision was made to send Father Olmedo and two others back to Cempoala with further bribes and a letter signed by Hernan and his captains. The letter stating that Hernan was the official representative of the king and any who did not join with him would be branded as traitors.

We made our move on the morning of May 28th. The rain that swirled around us was misty and seem to conjure up mysterious shapes that would loom towards us then drift away. Our progress through thick almost impenetrable forests was slow. Vines seemed to reach down from the trees to grasp our shoulders to pull us from our mounts, or twist around the foot soldiers ankles to trip them.

By evening as the sun set the sky on fire, we reached the banks of the Rio de Canoas which had been engorged with the rain which by now had become heavy and burdensome. Hernan gathered all the men to address them

"So my fine soldiers, after God, all that has sustained us has been your honour and courage. We will not surrender what we have gained with God's help easily. It is better to die a worthy death than to live a long life in dishonour. We will attack tonight, under cover of darkness before our opponents have the chance to realise we are even here. Glory be to God and Spain!"

His men were much inspired by his oratory and lifted him on their shoulders crying out cheers for him and for Our Lord. As he was finally lowered to the ground he gave his orders for the night attack. Sandoval would lead eighty of the finest fighters with the explicit mission to locate and capture or kill Narvaez. Diego de Ordaz would lead the largest group to assault the enemy positions in a surprise frontal attack while Hernan would lead a roving reserve to be deployed as required.

The horses led the way as we crossed the river. These wonderful sure footed beasts were so adept at finding their feet despite the waters that swirled around their haunches. The foot soldiers followed, the long lances proving invaluable to help steady the men and ensure a safe crossing for most. Only two men were swept away in the darkness, one of whom later rejoined the group, the other having presumably drowned in the black torrent.

Reaching the other bank, our passage hidden by the darkness and the constant noise of the now torrential rain, the sentries that Narvaez had placed were quickly overwhelmed, only one escaping to possibly alert his master. Hernan asked father Olmedo to perform a short mass to bless the men and sanctify the souls of any who failed to return. Before the final assault Hernan took me aside.

"Dona Marina, my invaluable love, I will not risk you in the confusion of a night attack. I bid you wait here near the river with some supplies. I will return victorious soon enough to rejoice in my victory with you."

I was anxious to be merely waiting, so often I had been in the thick of battle though well-guarded by Hernan's best men. I sat on a wet boulder with my only companion the page Juan de Ortega, straining my ears to hear what was about to happen. It was not possible to discern the passage of the battle by sound alone. No muskets were fired and all the fighting must have been conducted by sword and lance. There were shouts and war cries, groans and moans of pain and agony. It was all over in a few hours. I was delighted when one of the men came to me with news of a great victory.

"Gonzalo de Sandoval was magnificent!" The man exclaimed before continuing *"He and his detachment totally surprised Narvaez, they were on him before he had gathered his wits about him. Narvaez was wounded in his left eye by a lance and even now kneels before Senor Cortez in chains. Many of them gave up straight away and most have now agreed to join our force. In all we only lost a couple of men. Diego had sent two men to cut the saddle straps of their horses, and when some sought to escape by horseback they leapt onto their mounts and were swung ignominiously to the ground. Hernan implores you to come with me now to share in his victory."*

I followed the man, whose name I now forget, to the centre of the city. There I witnessed great celebration as the sun was just returning from its journey through the darkness.

Nearly all of Narvaez's men joined our cause. This swelled the number of men we could muster to over a thousand and just or even more importantly, our cavalry now numbered ninety six. As he had done before, Hernan ordered the scuttling of all but two of the ships. His iron will was manifest by his ruthless determination to go forward and never back.

We had little time to enjoy our victory. The very next morning a rider arrived from Tenochtitlan, rode stirring up a whirlwind of dust into the courtyard of Vera Cruz. His mount slathered in sweat and white foam encasing the poor creatures mouth. The rider was barely in better shape having ridden like the wind for many days. He immediately requested a meeting with Hernan, the captains and myself. His news was all bad

"Everything has turned to shit while you have been away!" Was his first statement before settling down tell us the whole story of what had been happening back in the capitol in our absence. I could tell by the look in the man's eyes that he was almost unwilling but at the same time compelled to tell us the truth. I remembered this soldier, Juan de..., I'm sorry Father after all these years his name won't come to my bidding. Despite having been given the opportunity to drink cool water and good wine he seemed anxious even to begin his tale. Sweat ran down his neck and glistened like little pearls on his forehead. At last he composed to himself enough to begin.

"I'm sure that everything turned even on the moment of your departure" he began addressing all the captains but Hernan in particular. *"The supply of food became less and less, and one by one the servants that had been attending to our every need seemed to drift away. There was to be a big festival that the natives wished to hold despite our presence in the city."*

At this Hernan turned to me for an explanation.

"The Festival of Toxcatl" I informed them, *"It is held every year at this time when the season is at its driest. Prayers and sacrifices of all kinds are made to Tezcatlipoca, the smoking mirror, he who sees and masters all. You will remember senor*

Cortes that you had agreed that those who had not converted to Christianity could continue with their beliefs. I remember this ceremony from my childhood visit with my father. A pure virgin male youth is selected every year. This chosen youth, called the Ixiptla, is treated like a king for the whole year before the ceremony. He is then sacrificed along with others so that his blood may ensure the coming of the rains."

I thought it wise not to describe in detail the sacrificial ceremony that I had witnessed from a distance as a child. I knew that the details would only inflame the blood of these soldiers of Christ.

Juan continued. Pedro had become increasingly concerned as the date for the festival approached. In addition to the changes in the behaviour of our attendants, some of the Tlaxcalans had approached him fearfully. They said that they feared for their lives as the Aztec had often taken their comrades prisoner during the Flower Wars and used them for sacrifices. Again Hernan turned to me for explanation.

"Every year there are mock battles held between the Aztec and all the other tribes. I think they are akin to what you would call tournaments. While some die accidentally, they are not real wars. They keep the warriors fit and their battle skills honed. The winners gain many prisoners, many of whom are used as sacrifices."

Hernan thanked me for my explanation and bade Juan to continue.

"Pedro toured the temples as the day approached. He saw many things that displeased him. The statues were all being freshly daubed and there were stakes driven into the ground. Our Tlaxcalan allies told us they were to chain our men ready for sacrifice, I know not if that was true or merely said to

inflame our passions. Pedro took three captives and tortured them to find out what was going on. Burning logs were laid on their stomachs and one was hurled from the top of the palace compounds as an incentive to the others to talk. Finally he got information that as soon as the festival was over there was to be a rebellion. He confronted Montezuma who claimed that he no longer had control over the actions of his people."

I could see that Hernan could tell that this tale was leading to some sort of climax and was anxious to hear the ending. He urged Juan on with his story.

"Pedro ordered half the men to closely guard Montezuma while the rest, including myself, were ordered to take up positions in hiding around the great temple. As the nobles and priests gathered for the final day of the festival and sacrifices and prayers began, we beheld a strange sight. All the participants joined in a strange dance that seemed to put them into a trance of some kind. As the dancing became stranger and stranger and more and more frenzied Pedro gave the order. The gates were slammed shut and he ordered our harquebusiers and crossbowmen to fire on the dancers. After the muskets had fired and the crossbow bolts flown we were ordered to draw our swords and put to death those who had survived. The Aztecs were terrified and tried to run but their exits were barred and many died being trampled in the crush. I have seen much my captain, but I have never seen so much blood flow in such a small space. The ground became slippery and we had to move with caution lest we slip and injure ourselves with our own weapons.

But by now we were under general attack from it seemed the whole citizenry of the city. We fought our way back to the palace of Axayacatl, Pedro himself took a stone to the head that caused his blood to run into his eyes. When we reached the palace we saw that the men who we had left to guard our royal prisoners had set about killing their captives. Only Montezuma and a few others remained. Pedro, blood streaming down his face and neck, went to Montezuma and held a knife to his throat ordering him to speak to the people and calm them. Montezuma and Izquauhtzin, the governor of Tlatelolco, were dragged to the edge of the plaza to speak with the mob that had gathered below. Izquauhtzin implored the people to go to their homes saying that the Mexicanas were not powerful enough to defeat the Spanish. This had some effect but we were now at war with the whole city. I was smuggled out of the palace and made my escape to warn you. I do not even know sir if our men in the city survived the night."

This was terrible news, but to add to the sense of woe, Juan added that the four small ships, the brigantines, had been burnt where they lay at anchor. Perhaps the loss of these potential winning weapons was the worst part of the news.

Chapter thirteen: Consequences

Hernan, as always prone to action, wasted no time in setting out for Tenochtitlan. He sent messengers out to gather back every available expedition that he had sent out to explore the country. As we approached Tlaxcala our force numbered about 1200 men including all up just over 100 cavalry. The journey up to our allies city of Tlaxcala showed me the difference between our battle hardened original force and the new recruits gathered from Narvaez's force. Our original men suffered the cold and the steepness of the ascent in stoic silence. The new men moaned and complained, much to the disgust of the veterans.

At Tlaxcala we were joined by about 2000 Tlaxcalan warriors, eager to put an end perhaps finally to the hegemony of the Mexica. This much enlarged force marched on relentlessly until we reached the city of Texcoco. Here we received news of the situation in the Capitol which I as always translated for Hernan and the captains.

"Pedro de Alvarado and his remaining men are besieged within the palace compound. They are receiving neither food nor water and by now must be in a sorry state. Montezuma asks that you come again at his invitation and he believes that order and peace can be restored."

I could tell at once that Hernan and his men no longer believed that Montezuma was of any use to them. Their belief, and the next events would prove this to be correct, was that Montezuma was a spent force and could no longer command his people. A part of me felt sad to think that this mighty emperor, as close to a god as any mortal, was now to be cast aside as if he were a broken implement. Despite his at times duplicitous nature, I thought of him as a man of great spirituality and dignity. I wondered what would now become of him.

So it was that on the morning of June 24th in the year of our Lord 1520 that we rode back into the city of dreams. How different this was from the other times. There were no curious crowds come to see our passage. The streets and causeway were not strewn with freshly gathered flowers. Smoke hung in the air and drifted slowly from the highest buildings. Our horses hooves clattered on the stones on the road, echoing through what seemed a deserted city. We moved as if ghosts in silence and in fear.

Most of our men were sent to quarters in a palace adjacent to the Palace of Axayacatl and Hernan and his leading captains came with me to meet with Alvarado. Pedro himself and all his remaining soldiers were close to the brink. Unshaven and gaunt they seemed shrivelled from hunger and thirst. Indeed one later told me that they had been reduced to scraping holes in the ground and licking any dark and slimy water that could be gained in that way. Despite their shocking condition they were overcome with joy at our arrival and their deliverance. Some indeed sank to their knees in prayer to Our Lord for saving them. Hernan wasted no time questioning Pedro about the events that had followed our departure from the city. When he heard that the whole crisis had been precipitated by Alvarado in response to the festival, which Hernan himself had instructed should be allowed to go ahead, Hernan shook with rage. I imagined that Hernan would punish Pedro severely for putting the entire enterprise at risk through his impulsive actions. It was not to be so. After a thorough dressing down the only consequence for poor Pedro was that he was demoted. My trusted friend Gonzalo de Sandoval was promoted to second in command, a decision I thought excellent, as Gonzalo had shown good judgement and courage throughout.

After Pedro had received his demotion I thought that Hernan would go at once to meet with Montezuma. I asked, *"Will you go now to meet with the emperor to see if peace can be restored?"*

"Visit that dog! He is useless, he has not even kept the markets open nor has he arranged provisioning for my troops." He replied, his face dark with anger.

At this Sandoval approached him and said that Montezuma had at least agreed to appear on the palace wall in an effort to calm the populace and that this had at least had some effect which may have resulted in Pedro and his men surviving the initial onslaught. Again his retort was savage

"That dog had been seeking to ally with Narvaez and form an unholy union against me. Now he can't or won't even allow the markets to reopen, why should I waste my time with him?"

Hernan's anger was truly frightening to behold. His men slunk back and said no more. I was not afraid though. For all his quickness to anger and his violence in war I had never felt threatened by him and indeed in all our time together he never struck me or even uttered a harsh word in my direction. Finally he calmed. *"Go to Montezuma and ask him to command that the markets be opened so that the men can be provisioned"* he instructed me.

Accompanied by Gonzalo I went to the chamber in which he was held captive. There my eyes beheld a sorry sight. The once great emperor stood manacled in iron chains to the wall. His eyes were downcast and his face was drawn and haggard. When I asked him to instruct the opening of the markets he shook his head sadly, tears streamed down his face and he replied softly that he no longer held power over his people and they would not respect his word. *"I cannot help you lady Malinche though perhaps one of the other imprisoned lords might have enough respect from the people to be listened to."* I knew it not at the time, but these were the last words I was to hear from this complicated but spiritual leader, who in the end had failed his people so miserably.

When I returned to Hernan with Montezuma's reply I once again saw his face harden as if made of obsidian. Wasting no time, he ordered that Cuitlahuac be released from his chains and brought before him. Cuitlahuac seemed willing to be of assistance and agreed to go to the remaining high nobles in the city and persuade them to reopen the markets and allow the provisioning of the men.

We were soon to learn that this was a mistake. Word came soon after that Cuitlahuac had indeed done the exact opposite of that which he had agreed to. Indeed he had betrayed his word and met with the nobles and exhorted them to attack and overwhelm us. So frustrated were the nobles with Montezuma's compliance with Hernan's wishes that his position as emperor was annulled and Cuitlahuac placed on the imperial throne.

When this news reached Hernan he again fell into a great rage, but as usual took action immediately. He ordered one of his best horsemen, Juan de Cordoba, to ride with all possible speed back to Vera Cruz to inform the garrison there of our situation. Barely an hour passed and poor Juan returned, horseless, bleeding and battered having failed to get away and being considered fortunate to get away with his life. He reported that all the bridges over the causeways had been destroyed and there were signs of a vast mobilisation of warriors.

Hernan quickly sounded the alert and set about organising strong defensive positions. The palace was soon transformed into a fortress. The Aztec warriors arrived in great waves. Muskets, cannons and crossbowmen all played their part in laying to waste the warriors as they surged like a strong ocean wave up the steps to the palace. In response the air became thick with stones flung by the Mexica slingers, the stones were accompanied by an equally thick hail of arrows and javelins. The troops had to hold their shields stoutly over their heads to escape this deadly rain or take shelter under whatever cover they could find. Some of the men were felled, falling dead or wounded to the hard stones of the palace. But for every Spaniard that was laid low a hundred or more of the Aztec were killed. Their dead lay piled ten or a dozen deep and became an impediment to others who sought to advance. Oh Father how the killing went on. Never before had I seen such carnage. At last night fell, and the roar of gunpowder and the raging of stones and arrows was stilled, to be replaced by the moans of the wounded from both sides that filled the night air. This horrendous slaughter went on for nearly a week, yet the supply of warriors prepared to assault seemed never to falter. For every one slain it seemed a dozen would step up to take their place. Hernan tried every trick or tactic he could think of. Mobile towers were constructed, to be dragged or pushed forward to provide mobile shelters for the muskets and crossbows. While at times effective these were not in the end decisive. The narrow streets surrounding the palace constrained the use of our cavalry who could not manoeuvre and pick up any pace, their hooves slipping in the blood that covered every surface.

In an attempt to halt the fighting, on the third day, Montezuma himself was taken, still manacled, to the edge of the steps, in the hope that the sight of their erstwhile emperor would calm the attacks.

As he stood there his head hung low he surely could hear the jeers of his once loyal people who then began pelting him with stones. The once great lord was struck in the head by several stones and Hernan ordered that he be taken back into the palace complex. The second to last ruler of the empire died ignominiously of those wounds that very night.

In the relative quiet of the fifth night of the siege, Hernan called his captains together.

"Brothers we must make good our escape tonight. I cannot guarantee that we would survive another day and surely if a time comes when our supplies of powder and shot are spent then we will all be finding our place with Our Lord Jesus."

With his usual forethought and planning he had instructed carpenters under the instruction of the ever resourceful Martin Lopez, to construct a portable bridge that was to be carried with us. The smelters had been at work melting down gold ornaments into bars. He continued *"Each man may take what treasure they can manage but remember speed may be our saviour and an overly encumbered man may rue his avarice. This is how we will be disposed... Gonzalo you will lead the vanguard with 200 of our most able soldiers, you will be in charge of the bridge and I also charge you with protecting Dona Marina, and fathers Olmedo and Diaz. I shall lead the bulk of our men and our faithful Tlaxcalan allies, while Pedro and Valazquez will form our rearguard. May God be with us!"*

Just after midnight Eli and I led Isabella, whose hooves had been wrapped in cloth to muffle their sound, quietly to the main gate of the palace to join our whole army and creep like thieves down the ramp and into the city. It was an unkind night with steady rain coming down, not the torrential rain of a storm but a steady unvarying rain that felt as if it might go on forever. The clouds obscured any light from moon or stars and we barely dared light our way with torches. The further we could get without discovery the better. When we had reached the bottom of the ramp I took Isabella's head in my hands and kissed her gently on the nose. We mounted, Eli behind clinging to my back, I could feel her body trembling as she held me tight. Gonzalo had detailed a dozen of his boldest and best to ensure my safety and that of the two priests. Porters moved ahead bearing the heavy wooden bridge that we knew may be the difference between salvation and death.

We moved like ghosts. An army of the dead, or perhaps soon to be dead. Making our way across the central plaza, wafting past the Temple of the Sun towards the first of the broken bridges that barred our way. The porters were gently moving our construct into place when a female voice cried out *"Mexicanas! They are trying to escape! Come quickly less they fall from our grasp!"* The deathly silence of the night air was then rent by an awful clamour of Conch shells and drums beating from the highest pyramid and then being taken up by dozens of other sites across the city.

The bridge was lowered into position and we began to flood across as best we could. In our haste all semblance of military order fell away. Soon we were spread out along the causeway like a ragged piece of string. Eli and I were now no longer at the head of the column having fallen back in the confusion. We were fortunate that Gonzalo's appointed guards stayed close and kept us safe. Canoes appeared in the waterways and arrows and slingshots soon rained down on our heads. Before we had a moment to gather our wits there were Mexica warriors attacking our straggling column from both ends and rising up from canoes to gain a footing on the causeway. Total chaos reigned. I saw two of the horses lose their footing on the slippery stones of the causeway and plunge helplessly into the waters below. Our men also began to fall to this onslaught, taking as ever many of the Aztec with them to pay for their passage to heaven. Oh how Eli clung to me and I to her. We both trembled with fright. The noise of battle, the clash of steel on obsidian and the cries of the fallen mixed with war cries and other wicked utterances from the hordes of attacking warriors.

At the next, and praise God last, breach in the causeway a terrible sight greeted my eyes. The gap in the causeway was already filled with so many dead bodies from both sides that it was possible to cross on a bridge of corpses. Truly Father I had no wish to tread on the bodies of the fallen but if we were to live, there was no alternative. As we struggled forward I could see many of the Spanish soldiers divesting themselves of their treasure as they went. Gold bars, precious stones and many other objects of value were desperately flung into the dark waters of the lakes to lighten loads and speed progress. I looked back and to my horror saw Hernan slip on the pile of bloody corpses that now formed the bridge across the second gap in the causeway. As he fell the arms of Mexica warriors reached out to grab him. Oh how fortunate we were that two of his men were quick witted enough to slice at the grasping arms and haul their leader, already bloodied and bruised, back to the relative safety of the stone causeway.

As a sad grey dawn began to emerge from the eastern sky, barely illuminating our way, we limped and hobbled our way into the city of Tacuba where we hoped to receive if not a friendly reception at least one not filled with animosity. As it was, the citizens of the city seemed to ignore us, staying indoors and peering at us through slats and hiding in the shadows of doorways. As soon as Hernan arrived he sought me out to check on my well-being. We embraced and though I could see his injuries pained him greatly, he would not be stayed from caring for his troops. Clearly Hernan was sorely injured but he none the less took immediate control of what was left of his once proud army.

He ordered a roll call. When it was complete the tally of losses was devastating. Nearly 600 of the men had perished. Three of the captains had met their fate including the valiant Juan Valazquez de Leon who had fought bravely alongside the severely injured Pedro de Alvarado who had led the heroic rearguard. Half the loyal Tlaxcalan warriors, totalling some four thousand, were missing. Just as devastating, many of the horses were gone and of those that remained not one was uninjured, in addition nearly all the stocks of the gunpowder that gives the muskets their fire and force was gone, and not a single cannon remained.

When this grim accounting was completed he turned to me and asked *"Marina, will you search among the wounded and others to locate Martin Lopez?"*

"Willingly my love" I replied and set about searching through the ranks of the severely injured who were laid out in one corner of the piazza, covered from the now burning sun by crudely fashioned sun shelters. And indeed it was there that I came upon the reliable Martin supervising the construction of these necessary shelters. Hernan seemed much relieved when I was able to report back that his much valued builder had survived unhurt.

Hernan seemed willing to take the risk of a daylight attack by the Aztec to give his men, particularly the many wounded, some respite after the night's trials. It never came to our understanding why we had not been continually pursued and attacked for surely given our sorry state we were at our weakest at that time. Surely the Virgin Mary must have smiled on us to spare us what otherwise would have been an inevitable fate.

As night fell we once again set off for the friendly city of Tlaxcala where we were confident of help and succour. As the next day dawned we were harried constantly by small bands of Aztec warriors. Hernan had organised the men into four squadrons, each a mixture of his ablest soldiers and Tlaxcalan warriors. Inside each squadron a group of the wounded were protected by the encompassing square of the uninjured. Progress was slow but finally we reached the valley of Otumba which meant that we were now only a few days march from the friendly city. As we descended into the wide plain of the valley we were met by another terrifying sight. Many thousands of the Aztec warriors were arrayed in battle order before us. In their centre were a group of finely dressed nobles including the new emperor Cuitlahuac. The battle that ensued was as fierce as any but unlike the night of our disastrous retreat from the city of dreams we were able to use our weapons most effectively. Wave after wave of attackers were beaten back by the stern discipline of the soldiers and the power of steel over stone.

I was riding right by Hernan's side at the critical moment of the battle. Already, though all were in some way injured, the cavalry had proved their worth on the wide flat plain. Here they could charge as a compact group with such force that they swept all before them. Seeing his chance Hernan wheeled his horse around and called to five of his captains, including Sandoval and Alvarado, to muster all available cavalry and follow him. Charging forth he headed straight for the Aztec emperor his raised sword glinting in the afternoon sun. This sudden strike caught Cuitlahuac and the other Aztec leaders by surprise. The horses quickly covered the ground between our ranks and their prey at great speed. Hernan himself was the first to reach the emperor and knocked him to the ground with the force of his charge. Juan de Salamanca, who was following closely behind, leant down as he swept past and impaled the Aztec leader with his lance. Almost in the same moment Juan was able to grasp the sun god standard that held much of the power of the Aztec warriors. With great delight Juan handed the standard to Hernan who held it high on his horse for all to see. The effect of this was truly miraculous. It was as if the Aztec army, which had been a raging sea about to crash down and drown us all, suddenly seemed to melt away and lose all heart for the fight.

And so it was, bleeding, battered and bruised, exhausted beyond the ability to even speak, that our much reduced force limped into the outskirts of the city of Tlaxcala. It was July the eleventh in the year of Our Lord 1520.

As we reached safety, stunned and numb from the horrors of the past week, Hernan slid down from his horse and was unable to stand. The closest of his men ran to help and helped him into the shade of the nearest house where he almost immediately fell into a deep sleep and was unable to be roused. One of the surgeons examined him and declared that he wasn't certain that Hernan would live. His skull was fractured in more than one place, there was a vicious, still bleeding, wound on one hand and one leg was swollen and purple. The surgeon called for boiling oil which he poured onto the bleeding hand to staunch the flow of blood. Hernan did not cry out but bit down hard on the piece of leather that had been placed between his teeth. Dressings were applied to the hand and to other wounds. The surgeon then daintily picked pieces of fractured skull bone from my love's head before saying that there was no more he could do for our valiant leader. Father Olmedo was on hand, clutching his wooden crucifix, ready to offer him the last rights to ease his passage to heaven should that be Our Lord's will.

I did not leave his side for six days. He slept. Not the restful sleep that might restore body and mind but a fitful nightmarish sleep filled with turbulent dreams that caused him to cry out. I bathed him with damp cloths to expunge the sweat that ran down his face and body. I changed his dressings, cleaned his wounds and did all I could to give him comfort. Oh Father how I prayed to the Virgin Mary and to Our Lord Jesus Christ to deliver him back to me.

On the morning of the sixth day he finally roused, opening his eyes and weakly gripping my hand. By evening of that day he was able to stand and using my arm for support was able to leave the house and walk slowly out to survey the condition of his men.

Chapter fourteen: Death by other means

As I helped him along he at first clung very tightly to my arm but as we approached the infirmary he gently pushed aside my assistance and walked slowly and tentatively on his own. The infirmary was a sad sight. Several dozen men lay on crudely constructed cots shaded under wooden roofs covered with thick palm leaves. Some were so weak that they were unresponsive, eyes either closed or staring into a far off nowhere. Some were sweating rivers, others had strangely cold clammy skin. Those that were able to respond seemed grateful for the visit and some even enquired after Hernan's own wounds. All in all it was a depressing but necessary visit.

As his strength slowly returned Hernan was able to spend more and more time attending to his army's situation and planning his next moves. He knew his men, while many were slowly recovering well from their wounds, were in low spirits. First he met with his Tlaxcalan allies and sought assurances of their on-going support, which after some internal debate they gave whole heartedly. With their support assured he turned to reinvigorating his Spanish army. Runners were sent down to Villa Rica to request whatever men could be spared and most importantly supplies of arms and in particular gunpowder.

As his preparations moved along he heard rumblings from some of the men, in the majority the later recruits from the Narvaez force, the general gist of complaint was that the expedition had now failed and they should retreat to the coast and perhaps back to Hispaniola. Hernan would have none of it.

He called all together and addressed them thus

"My soldiers, my warriors of Christ, listen well to what I say. Our struggles in Tenochtitlan were great and grievous, had it not been for the blessing of our Holy Mother Mary, we might

all have all perished. But we prevailed. Yes we have been defeated but tell me what great army in all of history has not suffered a setback on its way to glory? Never since we the proud Spanish people arrived in these Western Indies have we slunk away in fear. Do not let this be the first. Fortune always favours the bold and together we will still achieve great glory and riches."

This stirring speech went on for longer than I have recounted here, but the substance that I have spoken here, lingers in my memory. His impassioned oratory had the hoped for effect and we heard no more defeatist talk from the troops.

Having rested for nearly three weeks Hernan set about on another short campaign. On this occasion I did not accompany him for I was concerned for the health of the mother of my heart, Eli.

The morning of Hernan's departure to conquer the province of Tepeaca Eli did not come to greet me as usual. I left the bed I shared with Hernan and sought her out. Uncharacteristically, for she was a person who was always busy, she was still laying on her sleeping mat. She was sweating profusely with small rivulets of liquid running down her face and neck. Examining her skin closely I could see that it was red in many places and small bumps were beginning to appear on her skin. Leaving her briefly I went to Hernan.

"Hernan my love, Eli is unwell and I am concerned for her. She is not well enough to travel and I have no wish to leave her alone if feeling sick. She and I have barely been apart since we were reunited."

To my relief Hernan had no objection to my staying behind to tend to my dear friend. He said that though he would miss my wisdom and my skill with the nuances of many languages, that he could manage well enough with the help of Aguilar who had improved his Nahuatl greatly over the past few months.

Eli's condition seemed to neither improve nor decline for a few days. She remained listless and fevered. I stayed by her side seeking to cool her fever with regular bathing and applying damp cloths. On the fifth day of her confinement I noticed that what had at first been very small marks on her skin had grown into ever larger blisters. These blisters caused her great pain. To my eye they seemed not unlike those caused by fire or scalding water. She could not lie on her stomach and every movement caused her to cry out in agony. Soon I could not even dab her skin with a dampened cloth, I could only dribble water gently onto her blistered and burnt skin. Calling to the surgeon who had remained behind, I asked him if he knew what this terrible affliction might be. He examined Eli's skin careful and even sent a needle to pierce one of the blisters which immediately erupted like one of the smoking mountains spurting a foul smelling liquid into the air.

"This is very bad Dona Marina" he declared. *"She has an affliction called the red plague or in some parts it is known as the pox or speckled monster. I have seen cases of this before. It is a very grave illness that can sweep through a town or village causing the death of many who are afflicted. Even those who survive are marked forever by the passage of the affliction, their faces scarred and pock-marked."*

I was greatly alarmed at this information and begged of him to tell me if there was anything else I could do to assuage my friend's agony. He simply said that I was doing all that could be done and that he would happily pray with me that Eli be delivered from her plight. Together we knelt by Eli's mat, joined later by Father Diaz, and offered up our prayers to Our Lord, both Son and Father, to beg her deliverance.

For eleven days Eli lay thus, the fever neither diminishing nor increasing while the horrible pus filled blisters covered more and more of her body. On the night of the eleventh day my dearly beloved Eli departed this earth. At the end she suddenly seemed at peace. Her eyes were cloudy but the constant flood of sweat slowed and she was able to look at me. I took her hand and I swear by our mother Mary that at the moment of her passing I felt a lightening of the air in the room and a sudden feeling of joy. I cannot explain this but it was so. At the moment of my friend's death I felt a sudden feeling of peace and contentment.

I lit candles and held vigil by her side while Father Diaz made arrangements for her funeral which was to be held immediately the next morning. It was not until my friend was given a decent Christian service and laid in the ground that my heart broke. I would not be seen to weaken in front of those present, so I waited until I was back in our chambers to unleash the dammed up flood of grief within me. For three days I remained sequestered in the chambers I shared with Hernan, letting my tears flow unbridled, taking no sustenance and allowing no visitors.

Emerging at last, having dressed myself in a mourner's black garb, I sought news of Hernan and the 450 or so men he had taken with him to subdue Tepeaca.

The first of the men to arrive back with news of this expedition was a noble Spanish man called Juan Jaramillo with whom I had conversed before on a number of occasions.

"Juan, Juan, tell me of the expedition and also of Senor Cortes, has his health and strength been fully restored? Is he well?"

I was much relieved when Jan replied thus

"Yes Dona Marina, Senor Cortes is in good health and will be returning in a few days."

"And how did you all fare on the expedition? Have you brought the region of Tepeaca to heel?"

"Our men were victorious in every encounter with the Tepeaca fighters. At first Senor Cortes offered them the chance to lay down their arms and join our alliance but when they refused and even threatened to kill or capture our whole army he was made very angry. They even said that their priests would sacrifice any Spaniard or Tlaxcalan they captured and eat their hearts. This further enraged him and after hearing this threat he showed no mercy."

I was eager to hear of the events of the campaign and pressed him further for more.

"They chose to meet us on an open plain" he continued *"Our cavalry just cut them to pieces in every encounter, on the very first day of battle we killed many hundreds of their warriors without the loss of a single Spanish soldier. In subsequent battles he made good use of our war dogs who would leap without fear at enemies and rip out their throats before they could even cry out. These victories have buoyed up our men and restored their faith in our endeavour."*

It pleased me greatly to hear this news, I knew that the morale of the men was low after the retreat from Tenochtitlan and that a series of victories would do much to restore the hearts of the men. The night of our terrible escape from the capital was now referred to as "The Night of Sorrow" and had been the first time that our army had suffered significant loss.

Juan continued, though his next information was harder for me to hear.

"When we had brought the entire region to their knees Senor Cortes ordered that prisoners were to be taken in every town that had resisted us. The captives were brought to the central plaza of Tepeaca. Our blacksmiths created a brand with the letter 'G' to indicate 'war' and each and every one, women and children included, had the letter burnt into their cheeks."

I knew by this that Hernan was exacting revenge for the Night of Sorrow and that he wanted to instil fear far and wide. On many previous occasions I had witnessed his unbending brutality and harshness. When we had talked of this his reasoning was that by cowing his enemies through this sort of terror he would save lives later on, both Spanish and native.

Who can say if this was true? War is harsh and once it has been released onto the world its consequences cannot be controlled. Not for the first time Father, a war went on in my very soul. I had been part of so much death and I had acted as the hand of Hernan in so many ways. That night as I knelt by my bed I prayed to Mother Mary for guidance and help. I saw no miraculous apparition but woke in the morning feeling once again at peace with myself and my part in these momentous events. When Hernan returned from his expedition we did not discuss these matters, I was content to lay with him, our limbs entwined.

"I have a gift for you Marina, my love" Hernan declared.

Leaving our bed he went outside bringing with him a tall and very thin dog. This creature was most unlike the war-dogs that were kept chained at all times and whose fearsome aspect discouraged any approach.

My first response was most ungracious: "My closest companion and my substitute mother has died and you give me a dog!" I exclaimed churlishly. I could see that my response had hurt his feelings so I bit my tongue and said no more. When Hernan had dressed and gone about his business I sat on the edge of the bed. The dog came slowly over to me and gently sniffed my foot. Looking up at me with deep brown eyes it laid its head on my knee and just rested there. Despite myself, my heart melted and from that day to this Galga, as I named her, has been by my side. In truth there is nothing more dependable than a dog's love.

Our Tlaxcalan allies had maintained a wide and effective network of spies throughout the empire. Fast runners would bring us the latest news from Tenochtitlan, Texcoco and the other centres of Mexica power. Either I or Aguilar or sometimes even one of the page boys who had gleaned some of the languages would be called on to translate. It was the return of one of these messengers that brought the most terrible news from Tenochtitlan the very heart of the empire.

"What I have seen, no man should see. A terrible sickness sweeping through the people at a rate that I cannot believe" the man, Yaxcin, began.

"In the great city bodies are piling up in the streets, contorted and covered in the most horrible boils and pustules. The priests and medicine men do all they can to stay the course of this affliction but to no avail."

Father Diaz recognising many of the same symptoms as had taken our dear Eli from us asked me to ask Yaxcin what he knew of the first signs of the sickness, Diaz like the majority of the Spanish had learnt little of the Mayan or Aztec tongues. Yaxcin continued, *"It seems to begin with a high fever that won't abate for days and days. Spots begin to appear like raindrops on the skin of the afflicted. and these grow in size daily, causing immense pain and suffering. In some the pain and fever causes a state of madness and myself I have witnessed a victim throwing themselves in the lake in an attempt to ease their pain. In the end they become so weak that they can take no food and within a few more days they die."*

Father Diaz looked at me and nodded gravely, I knew he had no wish to alarm the others who listened, but I knew from his look that he thought this was exactly the same affliction that had taken Eli from us.

Indeed, soon there were many taken by its evil hand throughout our encampment. The Fathers and surgeons did what they could to ease the suffering but there was no effective cure. All that could be done was to try and keep the ill as comfortable as possible and await the outcome with prayers. Once taken by the great rash it was in the hands of Our Lord whether a soul was taken or not. I cannot say how many died and how many lived but it seemed to me that nearly one in three of our Tlaxcalan allies who showed the rash were taken. Among the Spanish men considerably less though many still suffered. Most of those who survived had deep pocks and scars on their faces that marked them for the rest of their lives. Every night I prayed to our Mother Mary that neither Hernan nor I would be afflicted.

Chapter fifteen: The ships that climbed a mountain

When this first wave of the pox had passed our fortunes changed. My prayers were answered and neither Hernan nor I caught the sickness at this time. Indeed despite grievous losses among our allies it seemed the sickness had been kinder to the Spanish than to all others. More good fortune came to Hernan in the months just before and after his victories against the Tepeaca. Hernan had left his most able and bold captain of ships Alonso Caballero in charge of Villa Rica. As our Lord would have it, several ships sent from both Cuba and Hispaniola as further expeditions of conquest were struck by storms and sought refuge in the relatively safe bay of Villa Rica. The daring Alonso was quick to round up any soldiers and provisions in these ships and bring them to our side. By this hand of fortune the number of soldiers was increased significantly and even more fortunately about a dozen horses were added to the cavalry.

I could tell that Hernan's heart was brimming with energy and confidence, he was more than restored to rude good health after his bush with illness. One night not long after his return from the expedition he called me to a secret meeting with the carpenter Martin Lopez.

"Martin, my loyal friend, I have an idea that may or may not be madness, do not be afraid to tell me if you think it folly."

Martin, stout friend that he was, just nodded and Hernan went on

"I now realise that we cannot capture Tenochtitlan by land alone. The causeways with their bridges mean that we can be bottled up in one area and assaulted by the Aztec from both the land and by the water from their canoes. If we can gain control of the waters then we will surely gain the upper hand."

Martin and I were intrigued and urged him to continue

"Is it possible for us to construct brigantines in good numbers at Tlaxcala and transport them to the great lakes?"

Martin considered this idea for several minutes before replying

"Yes sir, I think it is technically feasible. We would need to build them well away from the prying eyes of the Aztec, and then get them to the lakes covertly to gain greatest advantage. I would need to take apart one of the small ships left at Vera Cruz and use it as a model to copy, I was not totally satisfied with the four brigantines constructed previously."

His eyes seemed to glow as his soul caught fire with the idea. He began to speak more and more quickly, the words tumbling from his lips like water over a fall.

"Yes, yes, with our most skilled carpenters and many many porters it could, it will, be done. With your permission sir may I have the help of Dona Marina here to ensure the best communication with our Tlaxcalan workers?"

Hernan looked to me and I nodded though at first it seemed to me the whole scheme was the height of madness.

And so, for the next five months I was working as Martin's translator and assistant in this, the boldest scheme ever devised. First he sent word and one of his most skilled men down to Vera Cruz to take apart a damaged ship called a cog. The pieces of this dismantled ship were then painstakingly carried over the mountain by hundreds of porters to Tlaxcala. Martin and I were not idle while he awaited the arrival of the pieces of this ship. Hernan had already instructed that every piece of rope, every sail, every capstan indeed every conceivably useful item that had been salvaged from the sunken ships was to be sent and put at Martin's disposal. As these items began to arrive Martin arranged for them to be counted and their numbers put down on a great list. He and I, accompanied by two dozen workers and nearly a hundred porters, set off for the slopes of the nearby mountains.

There he instructed all to search for the straightest tallest trees of certain varieties that could be found. Of all trees he most valued the tree he called 'oak'. When one of the carpenters found what he thought a suitable example he would call Martin over who would then walk around the tree examining it from every side. If he was happy, then that tree would be cut down, and the best and straightest sections of trunk and bough would be sawn to lengths specified by Martin. For the men working the saws and especially for the porters tasked with moving this vast amount of wood back to Tlaxcala it was hard work. I enjoyed my time wandering through the forests and was very happy when I was able to call out that I had found a likely candidate. For the best part of a month we camped in the forests, the air on these lower slopes seemed fresher and more pleasing to the lungs than that lower down yet richer and more sustaining than the higher airs. As well as my own searching through the trees I was tasked with ensuring that all involved, especially some Tlaxcalan workers who had been trained in the use of a saw, understood exactly what Martin required. When we had gathered what Martin required we headed back to Tlaxcala, I with some regret.

When we had arrived back at that friendliest of cities, more complex, skilled work began. Using the pieces of the ship that had been taken apart at Vera Cruz as a model, Martin set about replicating it on a great scale. He proposed building 13 seaworthy ships that would give Hernan total control of the waters that surrounded Tenochtitlan and the other Aztec cities. I was fascinated to watch the process and to learn how and why each step was undertaken. Martin proved to be a good teacher, explaining each step with patience.

"Each ship is to be built in exactly the same manner" he explained.

"First we construct a frame that acts as if it were the bones of a person, it must be strong and true or all else will be out of shape and useless. Then the planking must be bent and connected to the frame with long iron nails, after this the decking, castles and mast are built, followed by fitting the rudder and all the ropes pulleys and other fittings needed to make the ship gather the power of the wind into its lung to propel it."

Despite this explanation it wasn't until I actually saw the ships being built that I understood the level of skill required. The carpenters worked with saws, adzes, hammers and mallets of every size, and other instruments to cut each piece of wood and shape it to its purpose. The bending of the wood for the planking was fascinating to watch. Fire and Water were used to bend the sturdy planks to the will of men. First planks were soaked in water for two days then they were put over a fire of hot coals that issued forth no flames. More water was constantly splashed onto their surface, escaping in a great hiss of steam to the sky. The wood was turned over many times until the supervisor was certain it was ready to lose the straightness it had been given by nature. Then it was bent and slid into a specially constructed frame and left to slowly dry to some degree. When ready it was a miracle to see it released from the frame and hold its new shape as if it had grown that way.

While this work was underway Martin ordered the damming of the Rio Zahuapan to create a small lake that the ships could be tested on. He asked if I wished to see the making of pitch, the evil smelling boiling black substance that was used to seal all the joints that might be exposed to the water. This was another fascinating process. Certain trees, called pines, were sought out and the sticky substance called resin that oozed down their bark was collected, sometimes a very sticky tree would be felled and the resin boiled out of wood chips. This would then be mixed with charcoal that had been ground up and the resulting mix would be heated up in great iron cauldrons. This produced the black foul smelling thick liquid that would waterproof every joining place on the ships.

By the time the first of the ships was ready to be tested on our little lake, I thought I knew almost enough to build my own ships if I had but a few skilled carpenters to help!

Everyone from Martin to the lowliest slave went down to the little lake to see the launching of the first complete brigantine. Martin asked Father Olmedo to bless the ship and hold a mass for all of us. Then the first of the ships, which to my honour had been named 'Dona Marina' was gently pushed and pulled into the waters. She floated perfectly, neither leaning to one side or the other. At the sight of this all assembled let out a great cheer and many whoops of joy.

It was sad to see the 'Dona Marina' hauled out of the water and taken apart, with each plank and beam marked with chalk and charcoal markings so she could be put back together later. But she had to make way for the next ship and get ready for her trip over the mountains to a chosen location near the city of Texcoco.

Hernan came to see how this remarkable endeavour was progressing and I could tell he was well pleased with Martin's achievements so far. They sat around a fire late into the evenings discussing the next steps in the campaign. As far as the next step for the ships goes, it was even more ambitious than the wonders that had been achieved so far. The disassembled ships were to be carried the fifty miles or so over the mountains to a chosen location about a mile from the lake shore at Texcoco. A canal wide and deep enough for the little fleet was to be dug so that they could be constructed away from the predations of the Aztec canoes until all was ready. After three days Hernan bade Martin and I farewell, as he now intended to rejoin the bulk of the army for an assault on the city of Texcoco in preparation for the arrival of the ships.

Martin and I at the head of an immense column of workers made our way slowly up steep mountain slopes and down the other side, only to be greeted by yet another peak to conquer. The strength and stoicism of the porters was amazing. Never once did I hear a man complaining as their backs bent under the weight of the timbers and they struggled to keep their footing on the steepest slopes. In this regard descents were more hazardous than the ascents. If one man lost his footing the whole load, porters and all, would start to slide and only men putting their own lives at risk by running to help could save the situation. It was thanks to the intervention of Our Lord that not a single man was killed and none of the ships' parts lost.

A rider came from Hernan requesting that I ride back with him to join up with Hernan and the main body of the army who were soon to enter Texcoco and my skills as interpreter and advisor were once again sought.

Arriving at the encampment about a half day's march from Texcoco I was pleased to see that Hernan was looking exceptionally strong and healthy, and his men carried themselves with the swagger of men who were confident. It was on the last day of the year of Our Lord 1520, that we rose early and completed the last few miles to this, the second largest city of the triple alliance once ruled over by the unfortunate Montezuma.

It was deathly quiet. Normally we would have expected crowds of citizens who were either there to greet us enthusiastically, or more likely in an unfriendly city such as this, to stare coldly at us and express their hatred and contempt in their faces. But on this day, the streets were deserted and we got no sense of any throngs of people hiding in their houses or back alleys.

"Pedro, take a couple of men and go to the top of the great pyramid and report back what you see" Hernan called out to Pedro Alvarado.

Pedro duly started scaling the city's highest point where he would obtain a great view of the whole city, the surrounding countryside, and the lake stretching out towards Tenochtitlan. Hernan called our column to a halt as he was wary that there might be a trap.

It took Pedro some time to make his way to the summit and just as much to return, the steep steps of the pyramid made going either way hard work, especially so for a man in full armour. At length Pedro returned and reported what he had seen

"The citizens are fleeing the city. All the roads out are clogged with men women and children making their way with haste to the countryside. But the sight on the lake was beyond belief, I cannot say for sure how many canoes are racing away from the city towards the capital, it could be seven or eight thousand, too many to count!"

Hernan was filled with anger at this report and ordered his men to seek out Coanacochtzin the ruler of the city. His men spread out though the city and could not find the ruler, interrogation of a prisoner informed them that Coanacochtzin had already fled. This did nothing to assuage Hernan's mood. He ordered that the few remaining citizens be rounded up and brought to the central plaza.

There they were branded with the well-used brands, women men and children alike. As had been his habit lately Hernan offered these captives to the highest bidders among the men.

For the next few days the men spent much of their time searching for food. It seems the inhabitants had taken nearly all the stores of food with them and had tipped most of what they could not carry into the lake. Our force of 600 or more Spaniards and our 10 000 Tlaxcalan allies soon ran through the scraps that were left.

At a meeting of the captains the possibility of departing from Texcoco was discussed. Hernan would not brook the word retreat, most likely because of the echo of the night of sorrows that still sounded deep within many of the men's hearts. Before a decision was reached, once again things turned in our favour. I truly believe Father that Our Lord and Mother Mary always intervened when we were at a low ebb. For how else can you explain that time and time again we were dealt new resources when were most in need?

Representatives of the nearby towns of Coatlinchan, Tenago and Huexotla approached and begged an audience with Hernan. These emissaries, even though they had assisted the exodus from the city, now begged Hernan's forgiveness and promised that their citizens would now help supply the city, and that they would encourage the return of as many of the city's citizenry as possible. Why this abrupt change of heart had occurred was not revealed to us. But Hernan was well pleased to now have safe and sustainable control of the second largest city of the alliance and have a base to launch his assault on the capital.

Over the next few months as the weather steadily warmed, Hernan and the captains were busy, as were Aguilar and I along with the few pages that had grasped some Nahuatl. Every day we met with leaders of surrounding cities and towns, making arrangements and alliances to spread and strengthen our position. I was conscious that I held a unique position and the chieftains looked at me with a look of reverence. From the reports of the web of Tlaxcalan spies it was clear that Cuauhtemoc was engaged in exactly the same work, trying to shore up his position before the inevitable, and maybe final, confrontation.

Hernan sent messages to the new Aztec leader in the vain hope that he might be able to persuade Cuauhtemoc to agree to a peace. He got no response. At another meeting of the captains he made it clear that his strategy was to gradually encroach on Tenochtitlan by capturing more and more of the surrounding towns and cities. Not until the ships were ready for action would he launch his main attack.

Hernan split the army in two, leaving the greater part of the Spaniards to keep control of Texcoco, under the ever reliable Gonzalo Sandoval, while he led a force of a couple of hundred or so and the bulk of our allies on forays into the hinterland.

It was on one of these expeditions that the Aztec showed their ingenuity and cunning. They would now rarely engage in combat in open spaces, having learnt the immense power of our cavalry. They had also adapted some of their weapons and tactics to enable them to fare better. In particular they now often carried long lances with sharpened copper tips that when used in mass were reasonably effective at stopping a head on cavalry charge. As always I was well protected by my own detachment of guards, tasked with keeping me safe no matter what.

We reached near to Iztapalapa, a beautiful city built mainly on stilts out over the lake. Here we found the most beautiful gardens filled with flowers and fruits with many brightly coloured butterflies flitting from flower to flower. Though nowhere near the size and scale of Tenochtitlan or Texcoco this small city had many perfectly proportioned buildings and temples. Its beauty only seemed magnified by the reflections in the still waters of the lake that surrounded it. Hernan remarked that this was where we had slept the night on our first approach to Tenochtitlan. So much had happened since that night, it seemed as if it had been a half forgotten dream. He ordered the bulk of our force to camp in a pleasant meadow while he and a smaller group went on into the city. I rode with him, as I nearly always did, and once again found ourselves marching through a virtually deserted city. We explored the city briefly and were about to turn about when Juan Jaramillo cried out

"Sir! Look!" He was pointing out towards the West of the causeway on which the city sat. To our amazement there was a wave of water heading our way. Not so large as to unseat us from our horses or submerge the foot soldiers but clearly something strange was happening. Within a few minutes water had risen to between the knee and fetlock of the horses and the infantry were struggling to move freely.

"Turn! Head for the higher ground!" Hernan called out and we made all possible haste back down the causeway to where the land sloped gently uphill. It was a close run thing, with the last of the foot soldiers needing to reach for the outstretched arms of their comrades who had already made it to the higher elevation in order to be saved. Once all were safe Hernan

turned to one of our many Tlaxcalan friends seeking an explanation. It seems that the Aztecs had dammed a small river then released the flood in hope of drowning our men. Once again Our Lord had plucked us from the jaws of disaster.

For the whole month of January small expeditions were made far and wide, gradually tightening a noose around Tenochtitlan while the arrival of the ships was keenly anticipated.

At last word came that the head of the column containing the ships was descending the final path towards Texcoco. It seemed every Spaniard and almost the whole population of the city raced out to see. And what a sight beheld our eyes as the first of the column appeared in sight. At the head were a dozen cavalrymen followed by hundreds of Tlaxcalan warriors who had all donned their finest cloaks and head pieces. As they approached the assembled throng of watching citizens, trumpets, drums and conch shells began to sound and the marchers began to cry out "Viva, Viva Our Lord! Viva Castile! Viva Tlaxcala!" I cannot say for sure how many warriors, soldiers and porters were in this mighty procession. Suffice to say it stretched back five miles from head to tail and took half a day to make its way into the centre of Texcoco.

Martin was feted like a returning hero and the city was full of celebration and gaiety in honour of the remarkable feat that had been accomplished. But there was to be no rest. All the ships' pieces were laid out across a vast field and carefully each piece was accounted for. Timber beams and the ship's planking were all to one side. Next were the tall straight masts, then miles of ropes all neatly coiled, then iron anchors, pulleys, nails and all the other needed devices. Last of all the big white sails were rolled up, laying like great caterpillars waiting to turn into butterflies and spread their wings.

Within three days Martin and his workers were hard at work reassembling the ships and starting on the Herculean task of digging a canal to the lake shore. Soon the canal site near Texcoco was an amazing sight for our eyes. Several thousand Tlaxcala workers were hard at work digging the canal that would take our brave ships onto the system of lakes. Father Diaz estimated that there were 40 000 workers, they were organised into shifts of about 8000 each who carried on the work day and night. The men, bare except for loincloths, worked cheerfully despite the at times difficult conditions. The sides of the canal had to be shored up with timbers as they went. I was not there to witness, but on one day the sides had caved and one man had been lost under the soil and clay that had poured down on him. None the less progress was impressive and Hernan estimated that the canal would be ready in only another two weeks.

When at last, after many weeks of toil, the canal was nearing the lake, we were greeted by good news from another Tlaxcala spy.

"The empire is in disarray. The new emperor Cuitlahuac had died of the sickness. The priests and nobles have chosen Montezuma's nephew Cuauhtemoc as the new emperor but he has not yet undergone the ritual. Many warriors and people have died from the pox and Cuauhtemoc is trying to buy as many allies over to the Aztec side as he can afford."

Hernan was truly pleased to hear of the empire's misfortune. I felt some sadness for all the suffering, having sat beside Eli in her time of sickness I knew the horrors of this affliction. He left the supervision of the reconstruction of the ships and the finishing of the canal to Martin and to Juan Jaramillo, who he had now promoted to captain to replace a man who had died of the pox. For he now turned to mustering his land forces.

Good news piled on good news, with further supplies, including the much-needed barrels of powder to replenish our diminished stocks and more men arriving from the coast. The support of the Tlaxcala was very considerable. Xicotenga the Elder had found his way to Our Lord and been baptised taking the name Don Lorenzo de Vargas, as had very many of his people who had joined the army of the saved. His support for the planned expedition was truly remarkable, he offered up to eighty thousand warriors to our cause! Hernan knew that it would be hard to feed such a horde and gratefully declined the full number, agreeing to take ten thousand of Don Lorenzo's finest warriors; he knew he could always call on reinforcements if needed.

For the next two weeks Hernan was away most of the time on his campaign to capture as many of the supply routes into Tenochtitlan as he could. I remained behind with Martin and Juan Jaramillo offering my help in conveying instructions to the chiefs among the thousands of workers. As the canal made its slow progress towards the waters of the lake the ships were put back together again. I could see the benefit of Martin's insistence that everything be marked and recorded when the ships had been dismantled. While all the ships were made from the same model I learnt that each one had its own nature. Unlike the iron of the anchors the wood was somehow still a living thing, and each piece for each ship would fit just so on the one it was part of, and not fit perfectly on another craft.

There was a constant stream of supplies and men arriving from the coast now. It seemed word of Hernan's successes, though strangely not of the Night of Sorrows, had spread far and wide among the islands. Ships and men had set sail from Hispaniola and Cuba to join the conquest. Juan and I were tasked with greeting the leaders of these groups and making them welcome while we awaited Hernan's return. We received word that Hernan, his men and the thousands of allies were assaulting the city of Tacuba, the third of the three cities that made up the triple alliance.

Among the newcomers was a remarkably dressed man. This gentleman was dressed not as a soldier but as a courtier. His clothing seemed to me to be most unsuitable for a setting such as ours. He was dressed in pale close fitting tights over which he wore beautifully embroidered pantaloons that billowed out then were tightened around his thighs. These were matched by a gold and blue striped undershirt made of some smooth glossy material hemmed at the cuffs with dainty blue lace. Over the top was a black jacket festooned with brass buttons and around his neck, just below a high lace collar he wore a richly constructed golden chain. Strapped to his waist was a thin, silly looking sword that surely was just for appearances, indeed it looked as if it would snap in two from a blow from a jade or obsidian weapon. He introduced himself as Julian de Alderete and in a pompous manner proclaimed that he was a representative of Charles the fifth of Spain.

Juan and I treated this strange visitor with all due deference but I could tell by Juan's manner that he considered the man weak and possibly a fool. None the less we clearly had best not offend the king's representative while we waited for Hernan's return.

Thankfully it was only a few days before Hernan returned. In private, with the captains and I, he told us of mixed fortunes in his forays. The Aztec had certainly learnt much over the last couple of battles. They now avoided fighting away from the water, using their canoes to escape if a battle turned against them. He told us that it was now very difficult to catch them on open ground where the cavalry were at their most fearsome. Again, we all could see the wisdom of Hernan's insistence on the hugely ambitious brigantine strategy.

When Hernan had briefed us on his actions he met with Julian de Alderete. I have never fully understood all the politics and back stabbing that went on in regard to the conquest. Suffice to say that Hernan had done a good job of keeping King Charles well informed and supplied with his share of the loot called 'the king's fifth." De Alderete informed Hernan that King Charles was very pleased with Hernan's exploits and that he was very much in favour.

Later Hernan told me how pleased he was that the king was regarding him so positively, it would help keep any rivals from Cuba or Hispaniola at bay.

Hernan took De Alderete with him when he came to see our progress on the ship construction and canal digging. Alderete was duly impressed declaring:

"Never has there been such an ambitious naval project so far from the sea!" I could tell by his smile that Hernan was pleased at the impression he was making with this ambitious plan. The ships were by now almost complete. Masts were in place though not yet rigged, and the 'castles' that would hold cannon, crossbowmen and harquebusiers were complete on the bows. When Hernan showed Alderete how the ships were being caulked to prevent the ingress of water between the planking he turned pale.

Having no access to the necessary trees to make pine pitch in this part of Mexico, Martin had turned to another method of sealing any gaps. First the gap was stuffed with cotton wadding then this in turn was sealed with a thick coating of fat. Human fat. It was extracted from the bodies of dead Aztec warriors and boiled to the right consistency and liberally plastered over the joints.

Hernan set off the next day on one of his now frequent forays to capture an Aztec controlled city where he would either wreak devastation or convince the inhabitants to come over to our side. Meanwhile Martin and I continued to supervise the last elements of the brigantines and supervised the pushing the canal to the point where it was close to breaking through to the lake. The Spring weather was unpredictable and there were at times great downpours that hindered some of the work but at least the waters did begin to fill the canal. During this time the wisdom of constructing the ships so far from the lakes was proven. An Aztec raiding party arrived on the lake shore fully intending to burn the brigantines before they could be put to use. Had the ships been closer to the shore this plan might well have succeeded. However, the Aztec had to make their way by night inland and were detected by sentries that had been posted and easily dealt with.

It took a further two weeks for us to complete the work but at last it was complete. The canal was opened to the waters of the lake and all was ready for their official launching. Gonzalo and Juan decided, quite rightly, that they should await the return of Hernan before the ships were launched. We waited impatiently.

After another three days word came that Hernan and his expeditionary force were close. Juan, Gonzalo, Martin and I rode out to meet him.

"Senor Cortes!" Martin cried out as soon as Hernan was close enough *"We are ready! Your fleet can now be launched onto the lake and play its part in the coming battles!"*

As soon as Hernan and his men had settled their horses, the last of the foot soldiers both Spanish and Allied had arrived, and all had drunk and ate their fill, we went with great gaiety to the canal side. There the ships lay waiting, sails and oars ready to breathe life into Hernan's dream of a navy on the lakes.

Chapter sixteen: Return to the city of dreams

The first of the Brigantines to make its way down the canal was the largest. She had been named 'La Capitana' and had been deliberately extended in length by the skilful Martin. She carried a large iron cannon in her forward castle and at the top of her mast fluttered the proud red and gold flag of Castile. Then followed the Dona Marina bedecked equally proudly with bright flags and heraldry, the remaining ships one after another followed. As each passed any given part of the watching crowd a great *"Hurrah!"* And *"Long live the Captain general"* as well as the usual cries of *"Tlaxcala!"* And *"Castile!"* Rang out. So it seemed as if each proud ship was carried forward on a wave of cheering.

When all were afloat and at rest on the lake Fathers Diaz and Olmedo performed a mass to bless the ships and their crews. Each ship was crewed by 25 men most of whom knew little of handling a ship but there were enough experienced sailors to ensure that each ship had one or two competent seamen. The complement of each ship consisted of a dozen to man the oars or sails depending on the conditions, a dozen or so crossbowmen or harquebusiers, and a captain of course. All among the watchers who had taken the faith took the sacrament, and now that so many of the Tlaxcala and others had found the Lord this took a considerable amount of time. At last when all had partaken of the body and blood of Our Lord we were blessed by a light breeze allowing the great white sails to be unfurled and filled with the breath of the Valley of Mexico. For the next few days the ships could be seen sailing up and down near Texcoco while the crews and captains learnt all the tricks and needs of each ship. I am told that each ship has her own personality and that each must be treated with love and respect by their crews.

Back in the city Hernan was organising his land forces. With the steady flow of reinforcements that had been arriving the force was now considerable consisting of nearly 90 cavalry, over a hundred crossbowmen and harquebusiers and more than 700 foot soldiers. In addition there was a huge multitude of allied warriors some say in excess of 200 000 but who can count such numbers with any accuracy? The numbers of fighters was so great that Hernan organised them into three land regiments and the naval one. He would take command of the naval forces with Martin as his second, and Sandoval, Alvarado, and Olid would each command a third of the land forces. The time in the great city that had ended in such disaster on the night of sorrows had not been wasted. Hernan had instructed that detailed maps of as much of the city as had been seen were drawn up. Every known causeway, canal, plaza and major building had been drawn onto parchment. These maps were essential in the planning of the final, we hoped, assault on the city. Each captain was charged with capturing and securing one of the great causeways that controlled access to the city, the naval forces would ensure that Aztec canoes couldn't land warriors behind the contingents and flank them. Perhaps the most crucial of the planned operations was the attack to be led by Alvarado and Olid on the aqueduct at Chapultepec.

Hernan's plan was to deny the city this most essential of life forces. We knew that there were a few springs providing potable water but nowhere nearly enough for the hundreds of thousands of city dwellers, let alone any extra warriors that had joined in the defence of the city. Hernan realised that if the defenders were denied water their strength would ebb and perhaps in the end their will would be broken. He was prepared for a long siege and had no expectations of a single quick decisive victory. Once again the control of the waters would seem crucial, for if held in his grip, the Spanish and allied soldiers could easily be supplied by the brigantines.

It was May 22 in 1521 when a final mass was held and the forces set out for their allotted missions. In effect the great city was to be held in a stranglehold until it submitted. The captains, Hernan and I had all agreed that getting trapped in the centre of the city as had happened before would be unwise. Instead Tenochtitlan was to be starved and denied the necessities of life until the Aztec emperor and his warriors laid down their arms and surrendered.

As the sun rose in the morning sky, Alvarado and Olid were the first to lead their contingent away from our encampment. Together they would seek to control the aqueduct and if successful Olid would then carry on to take control of the causeway at Coyoacan. Their banners flowed in the light breeze, their armour shone and their heads were held high, they made a fine sight as they headed off for this vital mission. The other captains, though rearing to be about their missions, were held back. Clearly if Alvarado and Olid couldn't take the two mile long aqueduct, or at the very least breach it, there would need to be a change of plan.

All day Hernan fretted. He paced up and down and was impossible to console. I knew him well enough that at times like this he was best left to himself for any intrusion into his brooding would oft as not bring a sharp response. I spent my day with Martin Lopez who was trying to impart to me the essentials of managing a ship under sail. I learnt that day that it was possible to sail against the wind using broad zig zag movements called 'tacks'. How remarkable that the ships could use the strength of the wind against itself!

As the sun lowered down into the sky and the clouds took on the colours of fire and blood we waited. At last in the distance a speck appeared, growing gradually larger minute by minute. At last a rider with news! The rider was my good friend Juan Jaramillo who had been given the honour of returning with the news. He had ridden hard and his horse's flanks were wet and there was foam bubbling around the brave creature's mouth.

"Victory my lords!" He exclaimed to the waiting throng of captains and native leaders.

"As we knew they would be, the Aztec were prepared to defend the aqueduct to the last. When we arrived near the water course a terrible rain of stones, darts and javelins poured down on us. Alvarado and Olid ordered our cavalry to dismount and us all to take whatever shelter was available. From there our crossbowmen and harquebusiers set about systematically thinning the ranks of the natives on the heights. Then when the rain of missiles from on high was reduced to a mere drizzle we were all ordered to charge. Even though the ground was broken and there were many large boulders acting as impediments, the cavalry were able to force the warriors at the base of the aqueduct to flee. From then it was easy for the infantry to scale the stonework and dislodge the last of the warriors on high."

"That is excellent news Juan!" Hernan exclaimed *"And has Olid continued on as planned to seize the Coyoacan Causeway?"*

"Yes, my lord and though I did not wait to hear for sure, our scouts told us it was barely defended."

Hernan took no time to bask in this good news but turned to Sandoval ordering to take his contingent to take the start of the city's main causeway at Iztapalapa. Turning to Martin he said: *"Well admiral Lopez, let's see what we can do with our little fleet!"*

With *La Capitana* leading the way the fleet set sail towards the great city. Well, to be accurate, it paddled its way towards the city as the wind had gone to sleep and the sails hung like limp rags on the masts. Hernan and I stood proudly on *La Capitana's* deck as the oarsmen worked hard to propel her forwards. Soon we came to a small inlet lying in the shadow of a rocky outcrop called Tepepulco. This place was familiar to Hernan and me as it was one of the places that the ill-fated Montezuma had taken us on hunting expeditions. At this time the outcrop was swarming with Aztec warriors who were busy sending smoke signals to warn others of our approach. Hernan was determined to extinguish this advance warning of our progress and landed a force of infantry to drive away or kill the signallers. From the elevation of this location we saw what awaited as when we were closer to the city. Several thousand war canoes cruised about in the distance, each one bristling with armed warriors.

The task of taking this observation post completed, we continued on our way, moving ever closer to the city that loomed large both in reality and our memories. As we moved closer to the city so did the horde of canoes to us. At last we were no more than a couple of crossbow shots apart. Hernan ordered the rowers to cease their labours and for a strange moment in time we just drifted, barely moving on the still waters. The canoes too ceased their paddling and it seemed as if both sides were drawing breath for what lay ahead. Hernan had ordered the cannons on the prow of each ship to be loaded and ready for firing. Matches burnt in the hands of the gun crews as they waited for the order to spit forth fire and death.

This strange hiatus could not hold. I and many others were mouthing silent prayers to Our Lord and the Blessed Virgin. And indeed it seemed as if our prayers were heard. At first gently then more and more steadily a wind began to stir the air, coming down from the high mountains and funnelling across the lakes. Turning to look behind us Martin could see the smooth waters of the lake losing their glass-like appearance and becoming ruffled in the distance. He turned to Hernan and nodded.

All at once the limp sails filled with wind in all their magnificence. Ropes strained to hold them to the masts and the ships leapt forward like bolting colts. At Hernan's signal match was put to powder and the cannons roared sending their iron balls into the massed canoes. The ships, like a cavalry charge, smashed into the frail canoes breaking them apart and tipping their occupants into the waters. The Aztec fired their slings and bows but these were useless. The missiles merely clattered against the sturdy oak sides of the ships and fell harmlessly into the lake. The air was made cloudy with the smoke from cannons and muskets alike and the crossbowmen were able to fire at will into the massed canoes. Soon the clear waters of the lake were turning blood red. The bodies of hundreds, or even thousands, of warriors floated like driftwood on the lake. After an hour or so of this slaughter the Aztec finally turned their canoes around and fled for the distant reaches of the lake. So it was that for the first time Hernan asserted his dominance on the sacred waters of the lake and proved the wisdom of his ship building strategy.

That night we joined up with Olid's land forces who had made some progress in fighting their way along the Iztapalapa causeway and had now entered the very fringe of the city affording more room to move than the narrow road. It seemed to me a strange twist of fate that we made camp for the night at Xoloco at the exact location where we had first met Montezuma.

As darkness threw its cloak over us we could hear the sounds of paddles in the waters and the calls of Aztec warriors echoing across the lake. Hernan and Olid posted a double guard just in case, though the Aztec rarely attacked at night. They were wrong, for indeed the Aztec were adapting their tactics to gain advantage. Already we had seen their use of captured or discarded Spanish swords and pikes, the swords often being attached to long poles to create useful lances. Not often now would they allow their warriors to be caught in open ground by a cavalry charge. Indeed on the narrow causeways the cavalry were of limited use and all the serious fighting was carried out by the infantry.

Around midnight the air was rent by the war cries of many hundreds of warriors who came charging along the causeway and others who tried to come ashore behind us from canoes moored up against the walls of the road. In the darkness it was impossible to see the shape of the battle and it dissolved into hundreds of individual melee making any tactical moves impractical. By first light it was over. The warming rays of the sun showed the results of that hard night's fighting. Bodies lay heaped along the edges of the causeway and others floated in the sullied waters of the lake. We had survived the night, and the cost to the Aztec had been large, though we too had suffered some losses but many orders of magnitude less.

Chapter seventeen: The long hard slog

The next few weeks were filled with an on-going battle that moved back and forth like the tides. During the day we would make sallies into the city and engage in some savage fighting. But despite their best efforts, the captains couldn't sustain a defensible position deeper into the city. During the night the Aztec would try and damage the causeways and dig pits that were filled with sharpened staves. Their slaves would labour building barricades and doing everything possible to make passage along the causeways more challenging. All of this had to be undone in the morning by our native Tlaxcalan allies, gaps filled in with rubble, barricades dismantled, all undertaken under a constant rain of darts stones and arrows.

Even on the waters the cunning Aztec generals had adapted their tactics. They had quickly learnt that the brigantine cannons only fired in a straight line and that they were slow to change their aim. The Aztec canoes now avoided massing in one place and when they attacked they zig-zagged to make it hard for the cannon to find their aim. To counter their improved naval tactics Hernan requested several thousand canoes from Texcoco to support the brigantines. The Aztec success on the waters combined with our inability to effectively use our cavalry, and the improved weapons that they had made using captured steel swords and pikes, resulted in a much closer result to many of the daily individual battles.

It was Alvarado who suggested the next strategy that we might follow to make progress.

"When we make our attacks our men are constantly under fire from the rooftops of the houses nearest to the causeways. We must burn those houses down so that they no longer have that advantage."

I could tell that Hernan was unwilling to destroy the city he admired so much. But Hernan was nothing if not an adaptable and pragmatic leader. After a few moments contemplation he relented and ordered that the brigantines be used to land small raiding parties whose sole purpose was to burn down the necessary buildings. For the next days a pall of smoke hung over this once proud and beautiful city as fires raged through some of the neighbourhoods.

On the morning of June 10th Hernan determined that sufficient progress had been made in preparation that a major assault on the city centre could be contemplated. It took all day for the Spanish forces to fight their way along the three major causeways to the city centre. I was with Hernan and the force under his direct control when we finally made it to the entrance to the sacred centre. As we stood before the eagle gate, its huge stone eagle peering imperiously down on us, a stone jaguar and wolf guarding either side, one more obstacle stood in our way. A massive breach in the causeway had been made by the Aztec. Not wishing to lose what limited momentum our attack had attained; Hernan was quick to order two of the brigantines to be positioned in the breach to act as a temporary bridge.

We fought our way right to the great temple. The priests were atop this mighty structure ringing bells and blowing on horns as a call to arms for the warriors to defend their most sacred of sites. Soon it became clear that despite our best efforts we were unable to secure a foothold in a defensible position and as the sun began to sink Hernan ordered a fighting retreat back to our base at Xoloco.

For a day and a night there was an eerie peace. It was as if both sides were exhausted and needed that passage of the sun to draw breath and lick their wounds. Our ever loyal

Texcocans had sent a further fifty thousand reinforcements and the arrival of this fresh force helped restore Hernan and the captains spirits. On June 15th another major offensive was planned. With the allied warriors in the van we fought our way through to the eagle gate once more. Here to my surprise Hernan called a halt. He ordered that we hold that position while every effort was made to make the causeway as strong as possible. Rubble and wood were jammed into the breaches and compacted down as hard as was possible. By this means it was hoped that the causeways would be harder for the Aztec to breach during the night.

This became the pattern of the next days. Hernan and the captains had perhaps realised that only a slow grinding incremental advance would win. So it was that day by day we crawled forward, constantly making the causeways harder to break and preparing for the time when the cavalry could be unleashed into the wide plazas of the city centre. Oh dear Father! How much death surrounded us. I wonder that the heavens could contain the number of souls released from their mortal bodies.

Our creeping advance had a most desirable effect. Cuauhtemoc, perhaps realising that he could no longer hold the sacred centre, withdrew his base to the markets at Tlatelolco. Alvarado and the brasher captains strongly argued that now was the time to set up our base in the city centre. Hernan would have none of it though. He continued to order a withdrawal at each setting of the sun, to be followed the next day by another thrust a little further into the city.

So far the impetuous Alvarado had been obedient to Hernan's orders. However on the night of the 20th of June, perhaps feeling over-confident from the steady progress his column had been making, ordered that his cavalry and about half his infantry encamp on the very fringe of the city instead of returning to their established base at the foot of the causeway. Barely had the cavalry unsaddled and tethered their horses when Aztec warriors charged them from three directions. Their camp had no natural or constructed defensive positions. Soon the camp was totally overwhelmed and close hand to hand fighting ensued. At closer quarters the advantages of the greater range of crossbows and muskets were nullified and the cavalry were caught totally unprepared. A slaughter followed and Alvarado and Bernal Diaz were both lucky to escape with their lives. Many Spanish soldiers were taken prisoner and when I heard this I set my prayers on this, for I knew all too well the fate that would befall them.

This sorry tale was relayed to Hernan by one of the brigantine captains who had been forced to stand idly by, his cannon of no use when friend and foe were so entangled, while the whole disaster unfolded. Hernan was furious, and had a letter written and sent conveying his displeasure in the strongest of terms. He did not however relieve Alvarado of command as I suspect he was also impressed at how far Alvarado's column had progressed.

When Hernan's anger had cooled he ordered a meeting of the captains which I attended. The captains were now always happy to have my presence at their councils and listened with appreciation when I suggested a plan.

"My lords, we have made steady progress into the city centre. But the devastation and loss of life has been great. Many houses have been burnt, many palaces and temples destroyed. Surely the Aztec must by now be feeling the privations of food and water shortages. I think we should almost every day send emissaries to Cuauhtemoc offering peace terms. I am certain that with the power of Our Lord and blessed Mary behind us

we will prevail. Cuauhtemoc may not agree to peace at first but as we continue to progress he may realise that he cannot win and thereby save many lives."

There was much debate amongst the captains, with some, Alvarado in particular, of the view that to offer peace was a sign of weakness. In the end the wiser heads of Hernan and Sandoval prevailed and it was agreed that every day an offer to cease hostilities would be made. Unfortunately the day for peace was not to come for some time.

Many more days passed and slowly the assault ground its way forwards, pushing Cuauhtemoc and his warriors into an ever smaller area of the city. None the less the Aztec resisted. In their wish to intimidate our troops, nightly ceremonies were held by the Aztec where captured soldiers were sacrificed to a cacophony of drums, conch shells and chanting. We could see even from a distance the sickening sight of captives being taken to the highest pyramid, there to be lain on a slab and their still beating hearts extracted.

Despite our overall progress, there were many setbacks and on one occasion Hernan himself was almost captured, only the heroic intervention of the captain of his bodyguard, Cristobel de Olid, saved his life. I do not know how we would have fared should he be captured or killed. I have no doubt in my mind that his leadership and personal courage was all that had held our enterprise together in the most difficult of times. It was after one of these setbacks, when several more soldiers were taken prisoner, that we heard that Cuauhtemoc had declared that within eight days we would be defeated and sent packing from the city. To reinforce this arrogant prediction our peace envoys were rejected even more emphatically. The day after Cuauhtemoc had made this proclamation our envoys, led by one of our staunchest Tlaxcalan chiefs and by the ever loyal

Sandoval, went forth to seek parlay with the Aztec. They approached and halted within calling distance of the Aztec positions. The Tlaxcalan chief shouted out the offer of an honourable peace where all would be spared if they laid down their arms or left the city. There was a silence and then five objects were thrown from the Aztec positions.

The severed heads of five of the captured Spaniards landed with a strange thunk, quite unlike any other sound. Their long hair and beards had been tied together and their eyes stared unblinking at us. At this Sandoval howled in rage and turning his horse away came galloping back to our position.

For the next eight days the Aztec attacks were relentless. It was as if having made his prediction Cuauhtemoc was determined to make it come true. The fighting continued from break of day well into the night. In those eight days we made no further progress towards the marketplace. At some point in the night the fighting would cease and apart from the designated sentinels, the rest of the men would lay down where they stood, still clad in their armour, resting their heads on any object they could find. There was no time for the niceties of life, like bathing, and barely time to gobble down the food brought to them by servants. The men relieved themselves near to where they fought and soon the whole encampment was filled with the foulest of odours of excrement combined with the stench of decaying bodies.

No doubt word of the fighting had spread far and wide into the countryside. The fact that we had made no progress for over a week and were just barely clinging on to what we had gained, must have been trumpeted by Cuauhtemoc and his allies. As a result word came that some of our more recent allies had changed sides again and were in revolt against us and our Tlaxcalan allies. This troubled Hernan greatly and he consulted me before assembling his captains.

"Marina my beloved, what am I to do? If we do not aid out Tlaxcalan and other loyal friends then we may lose their support too. But we are so stretched here I fear weakening our position."

I was by now well used to being consulted on military and diplomatic issues and contemplated for some time before replying.

"You must respond my lord. The Tlaxcalan have been the most faithful of friends. Many tens of thousands of their warriors have spilt their blood in our cause. To fail them now would send a message that we cannot be trusted in the most dire of circumstances. I pray every night for our victory, and I know that blessed Mary and Our Lord will not desert us now. Surely we are close to breaking the Aztec will. They have gone over two months now with insufficient food and water. We must keep faith in in our eventual victory."

Hernan had listened intently to this small speech. As was his wont, he stroked his beard and seemed to be staring off into the far distance.

I continued: *"If we send support it also gives the impression that our strength is greater than it is. If the Aztec see that we are not afraid to divide our forces then they will surely think that we have reserves aplenty to hold out."*

Hernan nodded on hearing this additional entreaty. He said nothing at first but came to me and fixing my gaze with his deep dark eyes finally spoke:

"Marina my beloved. You truly have been the most wise of my advisors and the bravest of all my company. I know full well

what fate would befall you if you were captured yet you have never feared exposing yourself to great danger. It was truly the will of God that you came to me, and I know that without you and the grace of God we would have failed on many occasions."

In the morning Hernan ordered Sandoval to lead an expedition to put down the revolt by the Otomi and other tribes. Despite our dire situation Sandoval was given nearly two dozen cavalrymen and a hundred infantry to march away from the city to deal with these revolts. Many of the captains thought this unwise but Hernan persisted having taken my words into his heart.

Not long after Sandoval and his contingent had departed we received good news from the coast. A ship had arrived in Vera Cruz carrying vital supplies including good store of gunpowder. Indeed our supplies of this most necessary of substances were running very low. Hernan had even sent an expedition to the top of Popocatepetl to seek sulphur from the very maw of the smoking caldera so that more could be manufactured. We soon also received good intelligence about the condition of our enemies.

Two Aztec warriors were captured in the fighting who seemed to be on the brink of madness. These once proud warriors were mumbling or shouting out in an incoherent way. When we examined them closely we could see their skin was drawn taut over their bones. Their limbs were trembling uncontrollably and their eyes seemed to bulge from their sockets where the flesh of their faces and heads had wasted away. I spoke with them kindly using the most polite form of Nahuatl and offered them some pieces of bread and roasted meat. They fell on this small offering as I have seen the war dogs consume their meals. They were given water which they gulped down with alacrity. When they had eaten more than was probably wise I questioned them about the condition of the Aztec forces. They described for me the most dire of circumstances. The warriors and ordinary citizens were reduced to eating almost anything- grasses, insects and even the dirt itself. Death stalked the streets of the city that they still controlled. Many afflictions were rife including the horrible pox that had taken my mother Eli and that I fear now stalks me. To hide their losses from us we were told that the bodies of the dead were being hidden in houses so that we could not see the extent of the toll.

When I reported this information to Hernan and the captains they looked pleased. My heart was torn in two at this time, for while my belief in Our Lord was unshakeable and I truly believed that we were saving souls with every baptism the priests conducted, it gave me no pleasure to hear of the privations of the inhabitants of this proud city.

Knowing that the resistance of the Aztec must be close to breaking, the captains and Hernan determined to go back on the offensive. For the next week our men and our allies in particular the Tlaxcalans renewed their assaults. As each day progressed it became clearer and clearer that even the strongest of the Aztec had been weakened to the point that they could barely fight. Indeed the battles were now very one-sided and the city became a charnel house. The stench of rotting human flesh sprang from the streets and canals causing us all to place cloth over our mouth and nose to ameliorate the smell. No longer did the Aztec attack at night and they seemed no longer to be able to destroy parts of the causeways. This enabled Hernan to make more and more use of the cavalry who could clear plaza and other open spaces with their terrifying charges.

Decades of enmity and hatred of the triple alliance fuelled our Tlaxcalan allies to pure savagery. They showed no mercy to any of the citizens of the city that were captured. Women were raped, men slain by sword or spear, and even babies were thrown up against walls to crush their tiny skulls. I implored Hernan and the captains to rein in our allies to no avail. Hernan stated that this was the natural order and that the Tlaxcalans were seeking revenge for many decades of tyranny. To me it seemed that the teachings of Jesus in the Testament were being forgotten for the fierce revengeful God of the old books. None-the-less Hernan continued to send envoys seeking a truce that might lead to a peace. But on every occasion Cuauhtemoc either refused to answer these entreaties or made an agreement to meet but then failed to turn up at the agreed place and time.

An omen came to light up the sky on what must have been the 75th or 76th night of the battle for the city. A bright light arose from the west and moved with great speed to hover over the city there it seemed to rotate as if someone had thrown a burning brand into the sky. Sparks and hot coals appeared to fly from the ends filling the sky with an eerie red and orange glow. All, friend and foe alike, stood in the darkness watching this marvellous sight and wondered at its meaning. Then just as suddenly as it had arrived the lights moved rapidly to the East and disappeared. Bernal Diaz, who had only recently had his own brush with death when almost captured during Alvarado's ill-fated advance, solemnly declared that this was a sign from God that our victory was nigh.

In the morrow every fit soldier and every brigantine was assembled for one last mighty push to destroy the remnants of resistance. There was little. Our cavalry and infantry raced through the few areas still held by the Aztec and swept all before them. The Aztec generals were all either dead or totally dispirited and resistance was only offered by small groups of starving warriors. Oh how terrible were the sights we saw that day. The streets we entered were full of rotting corpses. Even though we shrank from doing so, in places we were forced to walk over the bodies of the dead so thickly were they piled. The canals were clogged with the swollen bodies of the dead that bobbed hideously with any ripple as if they had been reanimated.

Our knowledge that we had at last attained victory was confirmed when one of the brigantine captains, Garci de Holguin, captured Cuauhtemoc as he sought to escape the city in a war canoe. Hernan ordered that Cuauhtemoc be brought before him so that with my assistance he could question him.

Cuauhtemoc was thin and pale. Clearly even being the emperor hadn't saved him from the privations suffered by his people. Yet he stood proudly, his gaze calm and steady as I translated.

"I accept that my empire is vanquished. My people have fought to the very end and all to no avail. Here take my own dagger and end my life that I might join the legions of the dead. This will put an end to the Mexican kingdom just as you have ended the life of so many of my people."

Hernan bade me tell the despondent emperor that he would not take his life and that he was sorry that he had not surrendered earlier and thereby saved many lives.

"For now, take rest and food. Tomorrow we will discuss the details of your surrender" Hernan declared.

Before retiring to his imprisonment Cuauhtemoc requested that his wife, who was Montezuma's youngest daughter, should be allowed to join him. Hernan assented to this request and so Cuauhtemoc and his wife retired to spend their first night in captivity.

In the morning the defeated emperor was brought before us for further dealings. Hernan was very interested to know what had happened to the vast treasures of the empire. He was told that the vast majority of it had been cast into the lake to save it from the Spanish. Hernan and the assembled captains took no pleasure in this news, one of the driving motivation of all the men was to acquire gold and treasure, for indeed they suffered from some strange condition that could only be remedied by gold. Hernan insisted that I pressure Cuauhtemoc to reveal the location of any treasures still in their possession. Cuauhtemoc ordered the few captured nobles to produce any treasures that they had hidden in the ruins of the city. The totality of this was paltry and not one tenth of the treasures we had seen in Montezuma's palace.

As a final request the humbled Emperor asked:

"Captain conqueror, I beg of you allow my people to leave the city in peace and make their way to other towns. My people are riddled with sickness and those who are not ill are either wounded or so weak from starvation and thirst that they can barely move. They are no longer any threat to you."

Hearing this entreaty and knowing the truth of Cuauhtemoc's words Hernan nodded and mercifully agreed that whoever wished to leave the broken city should be free to do so unmolested. I am ashamed to say that his order was not followed strictly by all the men. The next day citizens of the city began to pour out of their hiding places. Oh what a sorry sight! Men and women shuffled along with the blank stare of those who have gone beyond normal human endurance. Their bodies were thin and each one's face seemed merely parchment thin skin stretched over bone. Many bore unhealed wounds and most showed signs of one affliction or another. And they were not 'unmolested'. Many times the soldiers stopped passing citizens and roughly searched them in hope of finding hidden treasures. Any women who seemed in good health were taken aside and branded on their right cheeks to mark them as slaves.

Chapter eighteen: Peace

Now that our victory was complete Hernan ordered that there should be a great celebration in acknowledgement of the travails of the men. For 75 days the soldiers had been in constant combat and many had been lost while others carried the wounds of battle. Tenochtitlan was now no place to hold such an event so it was decreed that the bulk of the men would retire to Coyoacan to hold the party. The unfortunate captain Juan Rodriguez de Villafuerte was ordered to remain behind with a couple of hundred men to supervise the beginning of cleaning up the city. All the bodies lying in the houses and the streets were to be burnt and the lake was to be scoured for any corpses still afloat to be added to the pyres.

At Coyoacan a great feast was prepared. Hernan sent for many barrels of wine from the coast and food was gathered from far and wide. There was a small number of Spanish women freshly arrived from Cuba and along with a great number of slave women the food was prepared. Hunting parties brought in deer and turkeys while every available pig was slaughtered.

The celebrations soon got quite out of hand. The men drank wine as if it were water and they had suffered from a great thirst. Once well and truly in their cups there was no stopping their sybaritic indulgence. Men danced on tables while others dragged women, willing or not, to the sides of the room there to press them up against the walls and enter them. I could not stand the sight of such wickedness and retired to my quarters early in the evening. By the sounds that carried to my quarters the event raged on until nearly sunrise.

The following day few stirred as the sun rose and Hernan lay on the floor by our bed smelling of wine and vomit. When he had managed to stir he cleaned himself up a little and went in search of Father Olmedo. He begged the father to hold a mass to atone for the sins committed that night and give proper thanks to Our Lord for the victory we had won.

The question of the location of the great treasures they had seen still bedevilled Hernan and the captains. Cuauhtemoc was brought from Tenochtitlan, which was still smouldering from the funeral pyres, to be questioned by the captains. During our time when we first entered the city we had seen much treasure, none of which was now in our possession. The captains, with or without Hernan's consent, began to torture the poor last emperor of the Aztecs. He was tied to a great post that had been erected in one of the plaza, oil was poured over his feet and set alight causing the skin to bubble and split. Cuauhtemoc endured this with great courage and barely a cry escaped his clenched lips. Finally after two days of this and other despicable tortures he revealed that fearing their defeat the Aztec had thrown great quantities of treasure into the lake. Hearing this, Hernan sent messengers to Villafuerte commanding that divers be used to look for treasure and where the water was too deep that the lake bottom be dragged for treasure using fishing nets. Many bloated and swollen bodies were thus revealed but hardly any treasure.

What paltry collection of treasures that had been gathered were now divided according to Spanish law. The king would receive one fifth, Hernan would keep one fifth, his captains would share a fifth and the remaining quantity would be divided among the men according to rank and how long they had been part of the expedition. There were still several hundred of the original group that had set out from Vera Cruz so many months ago. As was their wont the most exquisite pieces of golden jewellery and artifacts were melted down into ingots for this distribution. Only the king's fifth retained some of the original pieces which Hernan hoped would pique the king's interest. When the ingots had been divided up, the share for the common soldiers was much smaller than all had hoped for. This once again stirred mutinous talk from many who had lost comrades and perhaps been wounded themselves. Frequently I heard laments such as: 'Why have we been through such privations just to receive this small reward?'

Hernan once again proved his ability as an orator by speaking to his assembled men thus:

"Soldiers of Christ and Spain! We have won a great victory! Already our priests have converted many thousands from their heathen ways to the light of Our Lord. I know full well that we have not gained as much treasure as we wished. But none-the-less we must remember one important fact. All the gold and silver of this fallen empire came from mines in the mountains. We now control those mines and can extract unlimited riches as our just reward."

Not for the first time I was amazed to witness his ability to hold the hearts of men in the palm of his hand through the power of his words. Indeed we both were gifted with great powers of language, his of persuasion, mine of my gift of easily acquiring different tongues.

To further calm any mutinous thoughts Hernan dispatched expeditions to as yet unconquered regions where it was hoped that more treasures would be obtained. Pedro de Alvarado was sent to the West where the great Pacific Ocean was known to lap on the shores; Cristobal de Olid was sent to subdue the still independent Tarascans; and finally the ever loyal Gonzalo de Sandoval was dispatched to found a new city south of Vera Cruz on the Gulf coast.

Hernan and the remaining captains set about planning the building of a new city, to be called Mexico City, on the ruins of the once mighty Tenochtitlan. For my part I helped the priests in their work of converting our many thousands of captives to the way of Christ. It was during my wandering among the Aztec captives that I heard the lament of the Aztec, singing of their great loss:

"Broken spears lie in the roads;

We have torn our hair in grief.

The houses are roofless now, and their walls

are red with blood.

Worms are swarming in the streets and plazas,

And the walls are splattered with gore.

The water has turned red, as if it were dyed,

and when we drink it,

It has the taste of brine.

We have pounded our hands in despair

against the adobe walls,

for our inheritance, our city, is lost and dead.

The shields of our warriors were its defence,

but they could not save it."

Father, I have indeed played a large part in the downfall of this once mighty empire. Tell me Father that I was right to throw my heart and soul into this cause.

It was just at this time Father that I felt the change in my body. Before even my monthly bleeding failed to arrive I knew. I chose not to tell Hernan for some weeks. I was uncertain of what his reaction might be. I knew that being right and proper in the eyes of the church were important to him. I also knew that he would never marry me. He saw marriage as just another instrument of statehood, to be reserved for strategic advantage.

Finally as my belly began to swell, and I knew that I could no longer hide my condition from him, I spoke.

"Hernan I am with child. Our child, God willing, will be born in the New Year."

Oh how my heart paused waiting for his response.

He raced over to me and held me in his arms, silently stroking my hair. At last he drew breath and spoke

"Marina my beloved, that is such great news! Let us hope we are blessed with a son who will become a great lord of this new country." Seeing my mild look of disapproval he continued,

"Even if we are blessed with a daughter I am sure she will be as beautiful and skilled as you Dona Marina."

It was on hearing this news that Hernan proposed the building of a permanent home for me and our future child. Together we chose a site on the outskirts of Coyoacan some eight miles distant from the new city of Mexico, close enough to be readily accessible but far enough to be free of the smell of death that still hovered over the ruins of Tenochtitlan. My house was as grand as many a palace, almost as large as my childhood home. I was to be attended by many servants, both male and female, who would take care of my every need. How strange Father that I should once again be a princess of sorts!

I lived in peace and quiet for the first time in many years. Hernan would come and visit when he could get away from his responsibilities creating the administration of his new kingdom. On these visits he would see the progress being made developing the many acres attached to the house and appreciating my good taste in the decorations. Often we would sit in the evenings as the sun went to its rest in the West, hand in hand, savouring a few moments peace together. My constant companion Galga lay her long elegant nose on my knee and seemed to be bathing in the tranquillity that enveloped us.

In reality these times with Hernan were few and far between. I never doubted that he loved me in his way. I also knew that he had many other women with whom he copulated. I also knew that he had a legal wife, Catalina Suarez Marcaida de Cortes, who was living on the island of Cuba and who he had not seen for three years. Day to day I spent most of my time with Patli, the head of my household, she whose name means 'medicine' was a very calm woman. Whenever I gave instructions in regard to what crops should be planted in our fields she would calmly listen and if she disagreed put her viewpoint clearly and simply. But in the end if I insisted, she would calmy nod and go about following my instructions. Together we made a good team and by the time my son was ready to enter the world we had the estate in good shape.

My child was born on the second day of June 1522. He did not come easily into this world and the pain I felt as I sought to push him from my womb was extreme. I was only wounded once in all the battles I witnessed, a glancing blow from a slinger's stone, but I have witnessed men in unbearable agony.

I can truly say that for two hours I felt more pain than I had ever imagined possible.

Hernan was away in Mexico City tending his affairs but when my labour began Patli sent a rider to fetch him. He arrived just in time to witness our son's birth. As I lay there exhausted, bathed in sweat but filled with an immense sense of relief, Hernan cradled our son in his arms. When Hernan passed our precious bundle back to me he smiled and said that he should be named Martin. This seemed fitting as Martin echoes the name of the Roman god of war and was Hernan's father's name.

The rest of 1522 and the entirety of 1523 passed in peace. Father, I cannot express to you enough how wonderful it was to be settled in a home of my own, supported by Patli and many loyal servants, raising my son. As before, Hernan came and went. He busied himself with the building of the new city and dividing the land amongst his loyal captains, each of whom was given substantial estates to reward their loyalty. This system of rewards was known to them as encomienda and as well as large tracts of land, entitled the captains to use the native people as servants.

I was not all that surprised when Patli, who had a good network of informants, said to me:

"Mistress, Senor Cortes' wife has arrived at Vera Cruz and is travelling over the mountains to join him."

How strange that this woman who had remained in peace in Cuba should now, when the fighting was over, be coming to join him. I tried to think little of it, her presence would not change my situation, after all I was the mother of his child.

I met Catalina just the once, for indeed as I shall tell you, she wasn't around for long. Our meeting took place in the palace of Coyoacan only a few days after her arrival. Hernan had asked me quite politely if I would be willing to meet his wife and would I kindly bring Martin along? I acquiesced as much out of curiosity as anything else.

Catalina was a very mouse-like creature. As is my way, I marched straight up to her to introduce myself and she responded but in a timid almost inaudible voice. I thought that she was not very pretty and seemed to hide her face under numerous veils that prevented a good assessment of her features. We sat next to each other at the subsequent meal. I tried to engage her in conversation, asking about her childhood in Medellin and her subsequent years in Cuba. In answer I merely got the curtest of responses. In the end I abandoned trying to befriend this strange reclusive woman and spent my time in conversation with Juan Jaramillo with whom I had formed somewhat of a friendship. At the end of the meal I made my excuses, saying untruthfully that I had urgent business to attend to at my hacienda.

It was only five days later that Patli came to me with more news, her network of informants was truly extensive, she would often hear things long before they became common knowledge.

"Mistress, Senor Cortes' wife is dead!" She exclaimed.

"How? When?" I responded.

"There was a banquet last night with much singing and dancing that went on until late in the night. Senor Cortes and Dona Catalina apparently had a fearful argument and she stormed off to bed early. In the morning Senor Cortes called his attendants saying that he had found his wife dead and tried to revive her."

Having witnessed more than enough of Spanish parties and having seen the drunken debauchery that went on, I was not at all surprised that they had argued.

"Senor Cortes' doctors say they believe she died from a weak heart, perhaps made worse by the thin air at this altitude but Dona Catalin's maids are claiming that Senor Cortes killed her with his own hands."

I knew well enough that Hernan could display a terrible temper but even so the notion of him strangling his own wife in a fit of rage seemed unlikely to me. This incident caused quite a stir but in the end the judges deemed that Hernan was not responsible. None-the-less for many months people gossiped and rumours were spread like the morning fog.

Chapter nineteen: Hibueras

I was granted two years of peace at this time. My life of quiet and plenty was once again disturbed by Hernan. He had been a regular visitor to my hacienda and took some delight in holding and admiring his growing son Martin. Sometimes when he visited I took him to my bed other times I did not. He did not seem bothered if I failed to offer an invitation; I knew he had many other outlets for his sexual energies. He kept me updated on his progress in constructing the new capitol Mexico City. He had brought in a Spanish architect, Alonso Garcia Bravo, to set out the plans for his new city which was to include his own palace placed directly over the ruins of Montezuma's now derelict palace. He now had hundreds of thousands of the inhabitants of the former Mexica empire working on the construction of many fine Spanish style buildings. But Hernan was a restless soul and even though the planning and construction was interesting to him, he still sought glory.

"Marina, my one true love, I need your assistance once again. Last year I sent the head of my personal guard, Cristobal de Olid, down to Hibueras to set about the conquest of that territory in my name. Olid has now turned on me and is claiming Hibueras as his own fiefdom. I have paid for his whole expedition and persuaded many of my loyal Tlaxcalan allies to travel with him in support. Now he has the gall to declare his conquests as being in his own name not mine!"

I was not for one minute flattered by his 'one true love' I know that he loved me very much but to declare me his one true love was clearly a falsehood, I was one of many. He continued:

"I need you to travel with me to Hibueras as my translator, my negotiator and my adviser just as you have been so many times in the past."

"Surely there are many others now who have the language to do your bidding in these matters?" I asked.

"Yes, there are some who speak Spanish and one or two Maya dialects but none who I trust as much as you Marina, and besides you understand the rivalries between the various potentates and can bring allies to our cause."

I was still unconvinced though I must admit to you Father that I too have a restless soul and the notion of another great adventure was attractive.

"Besides which Marina, word of your contribution to our victories has spread far and wide, I am told that some tribes even consider you a goddess!"

And so it went on Father, flattery piled on flattery. I know that I have a vain heart Father, and in the end I was swayed by his words and the prospect of further great adventures. I consented.

Our expedition departed on the 12th of October 1524. Hernan had determined that he could undertake this expedition with even less forces than he had landed in Mexico with. His army of conquest consisted of only 140 Spanish soldiers, nearly a hundred of them mounted, some artillery and a few thousand Tlaxcalan warriors. Along with the military aspect of the expedition we brought along about a hundred would be colonists who intended to find suitable locations to create new towns. Hernan's reasoning for such a small army was that in Hibueras there was no strong united empire like the triple alliance he had confronted previously. He believed that with my assistance he could use local rivalries to play one chieftain off against another and recruit substantial local warriors. Hernan decided to bring with him the captive Cuauhtemoc and other Aztec nobles for he feared that they might ferment an uprising in his absence. As it turned out Father he need not have feared this, there was more to fear from his own compatriots, but wait I'm getting ahead of myself. I fear that this fever is getting worse and muddling my thoughts.

When all was ready for a departure the following morning, a great feast was held.

That night when the servants brought us our food my stomach was churning and I was unable to eat.

"Marina, are you unwell? You normally have a hearty appetite!" Hernan asked.

I decided to hold no secret from him.

"My appetite has gone as I am again with child" I replied.

At this he was greatly pleased and folded me into his embrace.

"Perhaps Marina it is time for you to marry someone" he declared.

I knew full well that this was no proposal from Hernan. As I have told you father, he considered marriage as a tool of statehood, and while I had been of great use to him in the past I was in no way an advantageous prospect for the future.

"You must know that I will choose my own husband Hernan, I will not necessarily accept anyone you suggest!"

"Yes, I have no doubt of that Marina, you are a strong willed woman and I pity any man who be wed to you against your will. None-the-less I have a suggestion."

I merely arched an eyebrow, waiting to see who he suggested.

"I think it time that Juan Jaramillo should give up his bachelor ways, I have noticed that you two seem to get on well enough."

It was true that Juan had become a friend, was Martin's godfather, and seemed an honourable man. I did not love him and did not even find him particularly attractive, but he was kind and generous and could hold an interesting conversation.

It was at this farewell feast that I had an unexpected encounter. I have always paid attention and tried to be kind to those who serve us, I remember well my days as a slave or servant. As food was being brought before us I noticed a particular serving woman who kept her face obscured by her shawl and seemed to be going to extreme lengths to hide her face. There was something in her manner that awoke a distant memory from the labyrinth of my mind.

"Remove your shawl woman, I wish to look upon your face!" I ordered.

The woman seemed very reluctant to do so but finally unwrapped the cloth from her head which she kept bowed. I stood and walked over to her and taking her chin in my hand lifted her head up that I might look into her eyes. Then I knew her.

"Hernan, this is Cimatl, my birth mother!" I exclaimed.

Hernan then rose from his seat which in all respects was like a throne and came over.

"So this is the woman who sold you into slavery at a tender age! What do you wish to do with her? Death?"

I translated his words into Maya so that Cimatl would understand that her fate now rested entirely in my hands. She lowered herself down to the ground and began pleading for mercy.

"Get up, you have nothing to fear!" I commanded.

Tentatively she rose and stood head bowed, tears streaking her face, her hands working the cloth of her robe in apprehension.

"Malinali, my daughter, forgive me for what I have done, I have lived my life in regret since doing what I did. Spare my life I beg you!" She implored.

I found it interesting that she was not able to name her deed, maybe it was too much to expect a mother, even one as cold as she, to admit to selling a child into slavery. I very much doubted that she had spent much time filled with regret.

"I have no desire to have you put to death" I began *"I cannot understand how any mother could cast aside her child let alone sell her to slavers. I believe that your heart must be dark and full of an immeasurable selfishness. None-the-less I do not wish to have you killed. For I am now a Christian and follow the New Testament words of Our Lord that entreat us to forgive those that harm us or would do us ill. With Hernan's agreement you will be given to one of the Tlaxcalan lords who is now allied with our cause. I hope that you are treated well and that through this you may come to seek forgiveness by taking Our Lord into your heart."*

This was the final time that I saw the mother of my birth. I have never enquired what became of her but genuinely I hope that she lived out the rest of her life as a well-treated servant.

In the morning I agreed to take Juan as my husband. Juan had been kind to me, he did not have a temper and his main flaw was an excessive love of wine. I could do worse and at least this second child would be legitimized. Hernan sent for Juan to join us, Juan who had been given an important administrative role in the new city, was given leave to join us so that the wedding could take place.

It took us five days to make the march to Orizaba where we camped in the shadow of the volcano. No matter how often I have been close to such mountains I am always in awe of their grumbling talk and the smoke that issues forth from their summits. Truly they are doors into the fires of hell and I know well why they have been worshipped by many peoples. Juan had ridden out from the city and joined us though once the wedding was over he would return to his duties.

In an open field, with the mountain puffing out its steam and smoke, I was married to Juan. It was a simple ceremony conducted by Father Olmedo and followed by much feasting and merriment. I was able to partake in the feast as my stomach had by then settled. The next morning we set of for the lake at Peten Itza, some two or three weeks march away.

This part of the journey indeed took us the full three weeks. The countryside we marched through changed gradually from the high altitude fields to ever thicker jungles with small winding paths that often reduced us to single file. No longer was the air cool and thin and dry, now each day was hot and humid causing us to sweat profusely and was just as exhausting as the thin air of the mountains. We arrived at Lake Peten Itza in good order having only lost one horse that had stumbled and broken its leg, resulting in the decision to end its life with a quick slice across the blood vessels in its neck.

It was peaceful at the lake. The thick jungles reached right down to the shores of the lake making finding good camping spots hard. We made our way along the shores of the lake, which is about twenty miles long, finally coming to a suitable site. This site was a relatively open area with the ruins of some past civilization scattered about, as we made our camp the air was full of the calls of brightly coloured birds of various kinds who seemed most outraged at our presence. Perhaps their cries were in fact a warning about the challenges ahead.

We were barely a half day out from Lake Peten Itza when our troubles began. The path we were following that a local guide had recommended petered out and we had to resort to cutting our own path through the ever thickening jungle. Hernan sent scouts ahead to try and pick out the easiest path. He set out the general direction using his wonderful compass device that helped him keep us heading in more or less the right direction. Dozens of the Tlaxcalan workers and Mayan porters that we had recruited walked ahead using machetes to hack a path. This was such an arduous business that our progress was so terribly slow, after two full days we were only a few miles from the lake's shore. To add to our woes the air was thick with biting and stinging insects that seemed to delight in torturing us all but especially the Spaniards.

Day after day we slogged our way through the most horrible of conditions. Much of the time we were on swampy land and often had to detour for many hours to get around an impassable area. And it rained. Oh Father how it rained, not just gently but in incredible torrents that made it seem as if we were standing under the waterfall of some great river. At night we struggled to find wood that would burn so that we could light campfires to dry ourselves and our equipment out. The cavalry and infantry alike had long ago abandoned wearing their armour. The cavalrymen had their breastplates and helmets tied to the backs of their horses while the infantrymen entrusted theirs to the long suffering porters. Miserable and wondering when this insufferable journey would end we trudged onwards.

After over four months of these horrid conditions the jungle thinned out as we came closer to the cloud clad mountains that Hernan had said we needed to cross to get to the big lake on the other side. The path up through the mountains while more clearly visible was perilous indeed. It wound its way along the edge of steep precipices that fell away into thickly jungled valleys below. Horse after horse would lose its footing and go plunging into the valley floor below often as not taking one or even more of the men with it.

Men began to sicken. Some developed the sickness of the stomach where no food or even water will stay in their bodies, these poor souls soon became emaciated and as weak as kittens. Others developed the sweating sickness that the doctors called mal'aria as it was believed to be caused by bad air. I can only say that we were fortunate that none of our company came down with the small pox that had taken Eli and so many others. As we reached the highest points of the summit we were totally immersed in a thick mist that made seeing any distance in front almost impossible. The men held onto ropes or each other's shoulders and groped their way forward. Many men and horses lost their footing simply because they could not see which way to go. The descent from the highlands was no less treacherous than the ascent had been and when we finally reached the Lake Izabel we had lost over half the men and nearly all the horses. The rest were in a sorry state, few among us was not sick and all were hungry and weak from starvation. I meanwhile was now heavy with child; my pregnancy must have been more advanced than I realised.

We rested by the shores of the lake for two weeks to gather our strength. Fortunately the area had plentiful wild game and the forest was bountifully full of fruits. The lake itself was full of fish and it was easy to gather sustenance from it. The blacksmiths set about re-shoeing the remaining horses, many of whom were lame and all were in a thin pitiful condition. The Aztec prisoners we had brought with us had all survived the journey, I thought this miraculous, especially in the case of Cuauhtemoc who still hobbled from the torture he had undergone.

My daughter's birth came sooner than expected. It was the start of our second week at the lake and I had walked with Galga down to the lake's shore to take in the sights and sounds of the multitudes of birds that flocked there in the cooler morning air. As I stood listening to the conversations of many different types of bird I felt a sudden intense cramping pain. The waters that ran down my legs told me that like it or not my child had chosen this time to hurry her way into the world. I hobbled my way back to the campsite needing to stop frequently, bending over deeply, to draw breath deep into my lungs as a way of easing the intense pain. Arriving back at our humble camp I was immediately attended by the serving women we had brought with us. With their assistance I squatted and pushed the child from my body. This birth was every bit as painful as Martin's but considerably quicker. Within a matter of barely half an hour I was delivered of my daughter. She was a very small, frail, baby. A runner went to get Hernan. When he arrived he seemed pleased and briefly held her declaring with not even a hint of deception:

"Juan will be very pleased to hear that he is now the father of a beautiful baby daughter!"

I was glad that he would maintain this fiction and that the child who was baptised Maria Isabella Jaramillo would thereby be legitimised. Hernan had also promised me that at his first opportunity he would implore the king of Spain to legitimise Martin as his son.

On the day that Hernan had declared that we should depart the lake to continue our ill-fated journey one of his men, a cavalryman named Pedro, came to him.

"Captain General, I have learnt some of Nahuatl and while guarding Cuauhtemoc I have overhead him plotting treason."

Hernan was immediately alert; it was for this very reason that he had decided to keep his prisoner close rather than risk him fermenting rebellion behind his back. He nodded for Pedro to continue.

"He has managed to send messengers to some of the local tribes imploring them to set an ambush for you. He has promised them that if you are dead the Aztec in Mexico will rise up again and not stop until every Spaniard in the entire country is dead. When he has regained his kingdom he has promised them great quantities of Quetzal feathers and other riches."

On hearing this Hernan asked that I question Cuauhtemoc directly myself. I agreed to do so only if Hernan promised that the fallen emperor not be tortured any more. To this he agreed and I asked the poor man if this accusation was the truth. I knew in my heart that this brave an honourable man would not lie to me.

"In truth Malinche I seek to have my kingdom back. Would not your Captain do so were our positions reversed? Just as many cities had no wish to be under the yoke of my empire so my people have no wish to be forever under Spanish rule."

When I conveyed this to Hernan I could see that he instantly made up his mind to have Cuauhtemoc and the other three Aztec nobles in our possession put to death.

In the morning all three were hung from the sturdy branches of a ceiba tree. As he had been all along, even when tortured, the fallen emperor maintained his dignity and met his fate silently with his head held high.

Leaving this grim sight behind us, before the crows would come and feast on the strange fruit hanging from the ceiba tree, we broke camp and continued our journey into the dark heart of Hibueras.

Chapter twenty: The Honduran adventure

We made our way deeper into the interior of Hibueras. Hernan was aiming for the Spanish settlement at Nito, just across the Dulce river. Crossing the Dulce was no easy feat. Once again Hernan's foresight in bring carpenters and other artisans on the expedition paid off. The river was too deep to be forded, even the few remaining horses were at risk of being swept downstream. Camping beside the torrent Hernan ordered the felling of many trees called balsa that were known to be very light yet reasonably strong. These were cut to even lengths and carefully lashed together with vines and ropes. The challenge was how to get a light rope across the river which could then be used to pull over heavier cords and eventually hold the raft on a good line as it was paddled across.

"Hernan, I am an excellent simmer, you have seen me many times cross swollen rivers where many others feared to cross. Let me be the one who swims the current and takes the rope over." I asked.

"No I am not prepared to risk you, and beside you have just birthed a child" he replied.

I was disappointed, I have always wished to throw myself into challenges as they arose, but he was right, now was not the time to take the risk even though I was pretty sure I could manage it.

A Tlaxcalan warrior who had been baptized and taken the name Rodrigo volunteered to undertake the task. Rodrigo was a strong well-muscled man and came from a family of fisher-folk. Just as I did, he knew the ways of moving water and would keep his head regardless of the push of the current. If he was unable to make the other side there were five strong porters holding onto the cord to pull him back to our shore. Once the cord had been tied around his waist he plunged immediately into the water. Soon his head could be seen bobbing up every now and again, the porters played the line out slowly having been instructed to keep a little tension on the line. For a period of several minutes he disappeared and we all held our breath. Then he reappeared very close to the other shore but many yards downstream. We all cheered with delight. Rodrigo walked back upstream dragging the cord with him until he found a good strong tree to wrap the cord around. Hernan's men then attached a strong ship's rope to the cord and with huge effort Rodrigo hauled it across the stream. Once this had been achieved it was not so hard to get another rope across and use the two ropes to secure the balsa raft. It took an entire day but eventually even the horses, who were very skittish about getting onto the raft, had been transported across.

Feeling in a triumphant mood we camped on the far side of the river. In the morning we set off for the settlement at Nito which had been established some months earlier by Gil Gonzalez Davila. Our mood was soon deflated. When we reached the outskirts of the Nito settlement it was clear that all was not well. We were not greeted by any watchman nor was there any of the sounds of a bustling settlement. The small village of only a dozen or so crudely constructed houses seemed deserted, we did not even see a chicken scratching in the dirt. Our men went from house to house looking for the inhabitants. We found none and the mystery of the deserted village was not to be solved for some time.

"Hernan, this place feels wrong, this village has been cursed, let us not stay here but rather keep on our way towards the coast."

Hernan too could feel the sense of despair that seemed to hang in the very air in this accursed place. He ordered that we travel for at least another couple of hours before setting up our camp.

It was not until we reached the coast at Amatique Bay that we discovered the near starving remnants of the colony who seemed very pleased to see us. They told us that they had been unable to get any crops to grow and had soon hunted out the available game. The local tribes had offered them no assistance and indeed they had to fight many skirmishes to keep the local tribes at bay.

The settlers were given the choice of returning to Spain on the first ship that they could gain passage on, or trying to establish a new colony with the support of Hernan. Despite their desperate experience at Nito all but one agreed to help start a new colony in a fertile area called Naco. To ensure the safety of settlers Hernan sent the trustworthy Gonzalo de Sandoval ahead with a small contingent of soldiers to secure the fertile Naco valley. The rest of our expedition awaited the arrival of sufficient ships to give us passage to Puerto de Caballos since it was agreed by all that the jungles of the area were almost impenetrable. When at last ships arrived, we embarked for the relatively short voyage down the coast to Caballos.

The trip down the coast was very pleasant. There was a steady but not brisk wind following us, the seas were relatively calm and not a single cloud graced the skies. It seemed as if we were leaving our misfortunes behind and that from here on the expedition was to be blessed.

Arriving at Caballos it became clear that there were a number of Spanish factions vying for hegemony over that territory.

Hernan's reputation had preceded him. With very little resistance the Spanish hidalgos swore fealty to him and he declared himself the governor of all of Hibueras. Having decided that where possible we should travel by ship, the journey between the lakes having taught us a severe lesson about the challenges of overland travel, we decided to sail further South to Trujillo. Before we departed Hernan founded a settlement at a place he called Navidad de Nuestra Senora just a few miles outside of Caballos. During this time I played very little part in the affairs of the expedition, being called on to interpret when dealing with the local tribes, but otherwise having no interest in the machinations of what went on between the Spanish factions. Little Maria was not feeding well and my breasts that had provided great bounty for Martin were producing less and less each day. Maria distracted me from missing little Martin who had been left behind in the care of Patli and the other women at my home in Coyoacan.

The few months we spent in Trujillo seemed successful. Chieftains from far and wide came bringing gifts of slaves, quetzal feathers and other precious items, though to Hernan's dismay, not much gold. Hernan received these visitations gratefully and established good relations with the nearest tribes. He showed his wisdom by treating the tribes fairly and punished any Spaniard who stole from or hurt the local tribes most severely.

The colony at Navidad was not a success. When we had been in Trujillo for about three months the remnants of the colonists who had been left there arrived. They were once again in poor condition and dispirited by the difficulties they had faced in their efforts to establish a town. Once again their crops had failed to germinate and the supply of local game ran out far too soon. We had received word that Sandoval had been very successful in establishing dominion over the fertile plains of Naco, so these unfortunate adventurers were sent to join what sounded like a thriving settlement there.

My challenges feeding my little one continued, and I began to long for the comforts of my home in Coyoacan and my little son Martin. I approached Hernan and broached the idea of my returning to Mexico while he remained in Hibueras. He was not averse to the idea but before any arrangements could be made yet another situation arose requiring his attention and my negotiating and translating skills.

Messengers arrived telling us that the rulers of Papayeca and Champagua were massing warriors to strike against Spanish settlements. These towns were ruled by Nahua people and were one of the seven tribes of Nahuas of whom the Aztec were one. Seeking to avoid yet more warfare, Hernan sent messengers to the rulers of the two towns making it clear that he required their oaths of allegiance to him and the Spanish crown. These advances were soundly rejected and Pizacura, one of the pre-eminent Nahua chiefs went further and replied with a string of insults that referred to Hernan personally.

Hernan met with his captains and decided to send a punitive expedition to pre-empt any attacks by the Nahua. The force was small by the standards we have been used to in the battles against the Aztec, only a dozen cavalry, fifty infantry and a few hundred of our native allies accompanied Hernan on this mission. I remained behind, wishing to focus on Maria's health and live in peace in Trujillo. As these towns were only a dozen or so leagues away, we received regular updates on the progress of Hernan and his troops.

The messengers reported to us that Hernan had led a night attack on the Nahua town of Papayeca which caught the Nahua leader and his warriors by surprise. Capturing Pizacura, and also Mazatl in an attack the following morning, Hernan had quickly drawn the sting from this incipient rebellion. He had no time to bask in the victories. A ship arrived from Vera Cruz with news from New Spain and Tenochtitlan. A rumour had spread through the cities of the former triple alliance that Hernan was dead, predictably a number of the Spanish captains had begun vying to become the Governor-general of the territories. Despite not having achieved his ultimate goal- the conquest of the entirety of the central Americas, Hernan resolved to return to Mexico to deal with this threat to his authority and to show all and sundry that he was very much alive. Despite recent success against the Nahuas the expedition had not been as Hernan wanted it to be. Too many men and horses had succumbed crossing the mountains and several settlements had failed. In fact the Spanish hold on these new territories was tenuous at best, only the Naco valley colony seemed to be growing in strength. Originally Hernan was only going to return with a few of his resources but I spoke with him thus:

"If we return with insufficient strength your rivals may still consider that they can usurp your position. Let us return with all the force you can muster less what we have fought for over several years slips from your grasp."

I'm pleased to say that he once again listened to my counsel and we prepared to embark on all available ships to make the voyage back to Vera Cruz. A messenger was sent to Gonzalo Sandoval in the Naco valley instructing him to leave a small garrison there and make the arduous overland journey back to Mexico in support of Hernan.

It took three weeks to assemble sufficient ships to embark our full force but having experienced the overland journey we knew there was no risk of Sandoval arriving before us.

Finally we were ready to go. Hernan and I along with the bulk of the remaining cavalry and horses embarked on a ship called Santa Laura. Father Diaz told me that the ship was named after an abbess who was martyred by Muslims in the 9th century. It sounded as if she was a very brave woman as they killed her by putting her in a vat of boiling pitch. I know little of the Muslims but from the stories I've been told they are no more or less cruel than any peoples including the Spanish. At first the voyage North from Trujillo was as smooth as our voyage South but now we were on the cusp of the season of storms. On our sixth day all of this changed.

I was still struggling to feed Maria and was supplementing my meagre milk supply with sugar water. I was very worried about her. Soon enough I had more than feeding my child to worry about. The seas had been building all day throughout the sixth day of the voyage, The sailors told us that they worried that a great storm called a Huracan was building in our wake and it was this storm that was sending ever larger swells towards us. Looking back over the stern of Santa Laura we could see the blackest clouds that I had ever seen in my life. Though the wind had been building all day along with the swells, it suddenly dropped and for a few minutes the air was still but strangely heavy. The sailors were scampering around the deck putting any loose objects down in the hold and tying down anything that they could. The captain ordered that all but a small triangular staysail on the forward mast be reefed, which means the sails were to be rolled up and tied tightly to the cross-spars. I knew enough now about the business of these huge craft that they were expecting a 'mighty blow' and were preparing by reducing their sail area with just enough sail in operation to help keep the ship pointed in the right direction.

My only previous experience of a storm at sea was as a prisoner below decks. I never wanted to be trapped in the hold with water and vomit swilling around me, unable to see the sky and to breath fresh air ever again. I was determined come what may to ride this storm out up on deck, this was despite the urgings of Hernan and the ship's captain Diego de Almagro. At last they realised that I would not be stayed and allowed me to remain on the quarterdeck as long as I tied myself to the starboard rail. Poor weak little Maria I bound firmly to my chest using several lengths of cloth.

At first the wind was no worse than any I had experienced on land. But it didn't stop there. It built and built, becoming steadily stronger but also gusting with immense force every now and again, making Santa Laura lurch suddenly. The rain that accompanied the wind was not coming from the sky it seemed, but from the very sea itself. It struck my face as if I was being showered with a handful of small stones. Indeed I could not bear to draw breath facing into it and had to turn away to fill my lungs lest the force of air cause my lungs to explode. The crew could barely move about the deck as they sought to resecure any objects that had been torn loose. As one poor soul passed by on some task or another he looked at me with the eyes of a dead man, wide and fixated on nothing. I have experienced fear many times and I have seen men reduced to whimpering creatures by it. I know that look.

The Santa Laura was pitching up and down and I could see the Captain and his first mate both struggling to hold the wheel as it bucked in their hands with tremendous force. In the end they tied the wheel in the position they required, being unable to contend with the forces coming through the ship's rudder. As well as the rain, huge waves were breaking over the deck sweeping small objects and even men with them. I could see sailors desperately clinging to the railings or masts or any implanted thing that would restrain them. As I watched, one man lost his grip in a surge and was swept wordlessly into the churning seas. And still the wind blew. And still huge waves lifted Santa Laura up like a toy and flung her down again. The masts and cross spars bent and seemed as if they might snap.

I prayed over and over

"Holy Mary, Mother of God deliver us from this tempest! Save our poor wretched lives!"

So loud was the cacophony of waves, wind, and the banshee screaming of every rope and cord that I could not hear my own words as I spoke them. I did not know how long this went on for, it must have been several hours. Then just as suddenly the winds eased off and a strange calm descended. The sky was no longer totally black and there were gaps in the clouds not filled with the usual blue of cloudless sky, but by a strange almost glowing greenish yellow. I was about to untie myself and descend below to attempt to feed poor Maria but the captain implored me:

"No Dona Marina! It isn't over yet, remain tied to the rail and be prepared for more of this hellish Huracan."

De Almagro was correct in what he warned. Barely a more than a quarter of an hour had passed when the winds and rain returned, this time the wind coming from the opposite direction. Once again it was all I could do to catch my breath and use my body to shelter poor little Maria from this maelstrom. I was sure that one of the masts must surely break as they bent to the force of the wind. We endured more hours of this treatment, then almost imperceptibly at first, the winds began to weaken.

The Santa Laura rested on a gently wallowing sea. There was no wind and it seemed strangely quiet with just the rhythmic slapping of the waves on the hull to break the silence. I was sitting cross legged, untied, on the deck, trying to feed Maria as the sailors worked around me seeking to put right the damage from the storm. Hernan and the captain were conferring and poring over charts and examining Hernan's compass as they waited for darkness. It was clear that we had been blown well off course and by the absence of any sea birds we must be far from land. When the stars arose to fill the sky in all their glory they hoped they could set a course to return us to our intended path.

There was bad news. Our stores had been inundated by water that had washed down into the hold and even our fresh water supplies had been spoilt. How strange Father that after so much rain in the past hours, we now hoped that sometime in the next few days we would be blessed with rain! The captain immediately ordered that what little we had in the way of potable water and unspoilt food be carefully rationed. Lookouts stayed aloft scanning the horizon for sight of either land or at the very least of another member of our little fleet. They saw none.

For ten days we sailed on in a state of desperation. The crew were adept at casting lines and catching fish but our lack of fresh water was the real problem. We were not blessed with rain for the entire ten days. The men were reduced to having just a few sips of water twice a day while I because of my need to provide for Maria was permitted two cups each day. I was therefore in better health than anyone else on board. It is strange how every human body reacts differently to difficult circumstances. Some of the men went downhill very quickly either losing all their strength or becoming delirious and speaking incomprehensible words. Others, fortunately Hernan included, seemed to be able to bear the pain of the headaches and carry on almost as normal.

Faces became gaunt and sallow and most complained of a painful pounding in their heads. One or two seemed to be overcome by a fit, they lost control of their limbs and twitched as if possessed by some demon. Froth issued from their mouths and their eyes rolled back into their heads. When Maria was at rest I did what I could to assist the ship's surgeon in tending to the worst afflicted. There was little we could do for these poor souls except ensure they were shaded and give them damp rags to suck on. All of us were reduced to a dull torpor, laying in the shade and moving as little as possible. This strange soporific state was finally broken when a cry from the mizzen mast roused us:

"Land to starboard!"

Oh Father, how we rejoiced at those three words! Initially only a grey smudge on the horizon, the land gradually took shape. We still had no idea where we were, but at least land held the promise of a stream of fresh water. De Almagro ordered the lowering of a small boat that was loaded with barrels and sent ashore in search of potable water and any fruits or game that could be easily gathered. We waited anxiously, literally our lives depended on finding fresh water.

Late in the day, we saw the small boat rowing steadily back to the Santa Laura. Its crew wore broad smiles on their haggard faces and we knew at once that their mission had been a success. Rarely has water tasted so sweet, indeed we all imbibed as if we were tasting the sweetest wine that had ever been made. Along with full barrels of water the boat's crew had brought many fresh fruits and two deer that they had shot and butchered. Captain de Almagro kept Santa Laura anchored off-shore for the entire next day while foraging parties went to and fro gathering more of the much needed food and water. The following day we set sail North and within three more days we hove to just off Vera Cruz. Despite our success in gathering sustenance we were in very poor shape from the ordeal of the previous weeks. As I looked at my companions it made me sad to see their condition. All the men had a greyish sallow complexion and many had lost all their teeth. Skin was stretched taut over their bones and very few had retained any muscular strength they had begun the voyage with.

I rested with Maria in Vera Cruz for several days. Hernan went immediately to Mexico City to reassert his control over the colony which he did with very little difficulty. Once it was clear that he was not dead any plotters slunk back into the shadows where they belonged. Once I was feeling rested, and Maria seemed a little stronger, I made my way back to my home in Coyoacan eager to be reunited with Galga, Isabella and the loyal Patli.

Chapter twenty one: At peace

Oh how pleased I was to be back in my home in Coyoacan! The whole expedition to Hibueras had cost the lives of many men for very little in the way of achievement. Now that we were home, Maria seemed to gather strength and I no longer feared for her life. My husband Juan was completing the construction of a great palace and wished me to dwell with him there. I made a small effort but I had no love for the place. It was dark and gloomy with cavernous halls and shuttered rooms devoid of light and joy. I spend as few nights as possible there, preferring my own home. I have become very skilled at providing excuses that will take me back home.

Juan continues to drink more wine than is good for him. His face has become mottled and his nose red with prominent veins. Despite his drinking he is a kind enough father to Maria and I know that he loves her in his way. We lead our lives quite separately but when required we will attend ceremonies and feasts, sitting together and smiling a liar's smile. Oh Father you will think me a poor wife! But truly Juan seemed not to care that I would rather the company of my friends and servants than his. As long I was there when he wanted to show me off to visiting dignitaries he cared not what I did the rest of the time.

Father, pride has indeed been one of my many sins and I must confess that in these days I am proud of my elevated position in the new society. In truth there are no other Mayan or Aztec women who own their own estates and hold such an elevated position in the eyes of society. The Spanish all defer to me, and many of my own people avert their eyes when I am near, as though I were a divine or demonic presence. When dignitaries arrived from Spain or elsewhere in the Spanish Empire I am trotted out and paraded before them. The only blight on my life is that Hernan insists that Martin spend more and more time with him. I know that Hernan loves his son deeply and will do all that he can to have him legitimised and therefore be able to take his rightful place as his heir. But still I miss my lovely little boy when he is at his father's palace.

I have had just over a year to continue to improve my home and revel in the joy of being Maria's mother. Inside the house is light and airy but with sufficient shady verandas to keep out the heat of the Summer sun. I have furnished it in the main with furniture made for me by local craftsmen, though there are a few pieces in the heavy, dark, Spanish style. The fields around my home have been tilled and planted with maize and beans, all neatly protected by stone walls. I have even had vines planted and should I survive this sickness I will find a Spanish wine maker to turn the grapes into a fine wine. Yes, I know I delude myself. This sickness will take me soon, as it has so many before me including my real mother Eli.

I look down on Galga and how old she looks to me Father! Her muzzle is fully grey and she doesn't move with the incredible elegant swiftness of her youth. Yet I know she will outlive me, I know that Patli, who loves her just as much as I do, will care for her when I'm gone.

I give thanks to Jesus and his mother the virgin Mary for watching over me Father. For truly in the heat of many battles I could easily have been slain yet Our Lord has looked after me.

My time has come Father, and I beg you to say over me the last rites.

Bless those I leave behind and console all the sorrowful.

Commend my soul to Almighty God.

May I return to him who formed me from the dust.

May I be greeted by Holy Mary and all the Angels who will guide me as I go forth from this life.

May Christ who was crucified for me bring me freedom and peace.

May Christ who died for me admit me into his garden of paradise.

May Christ, the true shepherd, acknowledge me as one of his flock.

May he forgive me all my sins and set me among those he has chosen.

Father, may I join with you in reciting the 23rd Psalm?

The LORD is my shepherd; I shall not want.

He maketh me to lie down in green pastures: he leadeth me beside the still waters.

He restoreth my soul: he leadeth me in the paths of righteousness for his name's sake.

Yea, though I walk through the valley of the shadow of death, I will fear no evil: for thou art

with me; thy rod and thy staff they comfort me.

Thou preparest a table before me in the presence of mine enemies: thou anointest my head with oil; my cup runneth over.

Surely goodness and mercy shall follow me all the days of my life: and I will dwell in the house

of the LORD forever.

Epilogue

Dona Marina died sometime in 1528, though given the scarcity of records regarding her life after the conquest even this is not certain. The cause of her death is unknown but the likelihood of smallpox being the cause is high. This virulent disease is believed to have been brought initially to what is now Mexico by an African slave from Cuba. Accurate estimates of deaths are not possible but it is guessed that between one third and half the population perished. This is possibly similar to the toll brought about in Europe by the Black Death. History has recorded that after her conversion Dona Marina was deeply religious and I have used this in creating the artifice that she tells her story to a priest as she lies dying from smallpox.

The date of her birth is unknown but is generally thought to be around 1500. In those 28 or so years of life she lived a dozen different lifetimes. In Mexico her memory is in equal parts revered and reviled. Some see her as the bridge to the future and the symbolic mother of all Mexicans. Others see her as a traitor to her people. I have chosen to refer to her primarily as Malinali pre-baptism and Dona Marina post. The more common appellation 'La Malinche' is used as something of a derogatory term in Mexico in the form 'malinchismo' meaning someone who eschews their heritage and adopts foreign traditions and values.

In my mind the conquest of the Americas by the European powers was going to happen regardless. Had it not been the Spanish in 1519 or later, it would have been the English, Portuguese, French, Dutch...take your pick. The technological 'jump' that Europe had over the rest of the world as a result of the fusing of Arabic, Eastern and Western knowledge in the Renaissance would have ended in a similar result eventually. The Spanish conquistadors were hard cruel warriors, their courage in exploring and conquering vast tracts of the unknown (to them) is undeniable.

Despite the inevitability of the conquest there is no doubt in my mind that Cortes would have failed without Dona Marina's help. Recognition of her leading role in the Spanish conquest of 'the Americas' beyond the shores of Mexico is long overdue.

Sean Wheeler
Ōtautahi/Christchurch
Aotearoa/New Zealand
2023.

Made in the USA
Columbia, SC
26 November 2024

47246730R00140